Push

Events in this book are true, but names and locations have been changed.

We've been asked to see her,' the man said quietly.

'Don't worry.'

Down the stairs comes a child who looks like an angel.

And screams. And kicks. And shrieks. And runs away.

And swears at teachers. And abuses other children.

And won't eat. And won't get up. And hides in drawers.

And threatens you with a knife.

And has no concept of danger.

And wants to die.

PUSH is an account of denial, desperation,
disappointment – and finally, determination.

It's the way I got help with my mentally ill child.

Just push.

ISBN 1527208982

Push

Juliette Mare

2015

From the bottom of the stairs, I call her. In my voice there's sweetness, welcome, happiness.

'CHLOË!'

'SHUUUT! YAAH!' Bang. 'JUST SHUDDUUUUP! I'M GETTINGUPSOJUSTSTOP GETTINGONMY BACK WILLYA!'

'It's twelve o'cl—'

'SHADDUUUP!AYAMYAAH! I'M GETTING DRESSED. SHUT UP!'

She's deafening. I go back to the kitchen. My ears are ringing. The dogs are huddled together in one basket. The new baby sleeps, undisturbed.

Somebody has to help me with this.

Her brother's away at university. My mother's got cancer.

My daughter is thirteen.

Please will somebody help me.

+++

2010

She was eight when her third primary school asked me to take her to 'see somebody'.

Those first three schools were a pain. Teachers were always cornering me at the school gate. 'Chloë screamed' at them. 'Chloë kicked.'

'Chloë scrawled BUM-FACE right across the blackboard before I was in.'

'Well, she does play up,' I'd say, 'but so do a lot of kids. I was highly strung at that age. She'll grow out of it.'

Right now she was somewhere in the playground outside. All the kids were running about; I could see them but it was quiet in here. The school had 'invited me to discuss Chloë's behaviour' and her teacher, an earnest-looking older woman, thought Chloë might have ADHD.

'Attention deficit hyperactivity disorder,' she added, in case I'd never heard of it.

'You mean, she can't concentrate and climbs on the furniture?' I said, in disbelief. 'She's *eight*. That's normal. Of course she's active – she's ridden a pony since she was three, she's fearless. She concentrates well enough when she's interested.'

'She's uncooperative. You know a fire alarm went off and I couldn't get her to leave. That's a safety issue, Mrs Mare.'

'Miss Mare. Well, she can get bored. I'm sorry, but just because she tries it on doesn't mean she's ill.'

I could see exactly what the problem was. Teachers just weren't used to kids like Chloë who expected a high level of stimulation. That's why she always played them up, out of mischief. But the school insisted that I should have her 'observed' so I ended up driving her to see a paediatrician in a town twenty miles away. He asked about the birth (normal), babyhood (normal), kindergarten ...

'I've been through all this before,' I told him. 'She's always been a bit of a handful.' He was a burly red-faced fellow; he looked more like a farmer than a doctor. 'I'm not about to start treating my daughter as if she's sick just because she can be a bloody nuisance. I was a mouthy kid myself. But I manage to run a night-club and a livery yard and still look after Joe and Chloë perfectly well.'

He made notes on his computer. Chloë was quietly listening, swinging her legs a bit, not sliding off the chair or wriggling or kicking as she might if she was bored. She got up and went to inspect the toys in the corner. The doctor looked at me.

'So, as far as you're concerned, no problem. The teachers are exaggerating. Why would they do that?'

'Well – okay, yes, with me she's too clingy. I mean – when she's home, I never get any peace. She's always in my face, if I'm trying to make a phone call or something. But she's *eight*.'

'How would you feel – I'm not saying it's necessary, but how would you feel about some psychiatric help for her?'

'No! No, that'd be way over the top.'

The nurse took Chloë into another room for some tests and the paediatrician talked to me about 'parenting style' and adjustments to our 'lifestyle'. I was never to shout or smack in any circumstances and I was to read to her more, be around more, to make her feel safer. I took this seriously enough to give up the nightclub that had brought in most of my income.

I saw the letter he wrote afterwards, all about behavioural management and how I'd been advised to avoid confrontation with Chloë and how she probably wouldn't need other treatment right now. The teachers would have to take 'a nurturing approach' as well.

She didn't change. In the end I had to move her to a different school (again). I knew she was gobby and liked to fling herself about rather than sit still. But she was funny and curious and a quick learner when she set her mind to it. She did make most of the noise in the house, but then her brother had always been quiet and studious. I was looking after the pets and the stables and exercising our horse and taking him to shows so there was always something going on; that's what she was used to. Yes, she could be hard work, but she'd be fine. All I wanted was to protect my children, keep them safe and not put labels on them.

+++

2014

Chloë kept up academically at secondary school but at home, in the yard, she'd become unmanageable. I supposed she'd grow out of it, but at that time she shouted and behaved so obsessively around other people that I couldn't cope with her. She demanded as much attention as a toddler. I gave up running the livery stable, got rid of the eighteen acres I'd had, and sent my own horse to be cared for someone else's yard, which cost a lot.

Letters started arriving from the school. 'Disruptive' was a favourite word. It covered lying down and refusing to move, walking out of the class, telling teachers they were useless, arguing and getting into a blinding rage and swearing. I'd gone to a private girls' school in central London, and none of us would have dreamed of swearing, never mind being rude to teachers. But then I'd always believed kids were different at state schools. They were freer; it was a different environment. I told myself this, but the teachers wanted me to get advice from our GP, so I thought 'here we go again' and took her to the surgery. I showed him the letters.

Chloë, aged twelve, sat beside me, watching him. He said, 'What do you think, Chloë? Why d'you think you keep getting into trouble?'

'They tell me to do stupid things.'

'What things?'

'USELESS things. I mean if I'm not gonna learn anything like *useful*, and *interesting*, that I want to know, what's the point? But if you get up and go out, the teachers are pathetic. They just keep ON and on and on and on and —'

'What about your brother, d'you miss him now he's gone to university?'

'No. He comes home sometimes.'

'And you're going to have a new baby sister soon. Are you looking forward to that?'

'I don't think about it.'

He typed something into his computer. 'Well, we've got to sort this out for everybody's sake, Chloë. I'd like you to see a professional at the Child and Adolescent service. They're specialists. Are you happy with that, Juliette?'

'Yes. I want a referral. We need to see somebody.'

It was true; I knew that now. Joe had gone off to medical school in London a couple of weeks after Chloë started her second year and... I didn't know why, but she'd been more aggressive and demanding towards me ever since.

Child and Adolescent Mental Health Services were an hour away by car. I waited for an appointment, but when the letter came it was a refusal. We wouldn't be seeing a specialist because somebody in the NHS, some bureaucrat, decided my daughter didn't need to be referred.

+++

2015

I changed my mind about the horse. I couldn't pay somebody else to keep him forever, so in the New Year I took six acres, got him back and took other people's horses into the stables as before.

In February I drove Chloë to the GP. Same prompt (the school). Every other day she seemed to be in detention for shouting at teachers, walking out – they were demanding that I take her to the doctor again.

This time I'd push. I'd *insist* on somebody seeing us. Not because I thought she was mentally ill. There was no mental illness in our family. Nobody'd ever even mentioned it. I didn't know anybody like that. I just needed somebody to tell me how to handle my daughter. Maybe it was because she'd started her periods. Hormones or something. Because she was impossible.

'Come on Chloë, it's bedtime.'

'I'm BUSY, CAN'T YOU FUCKING SEE?'

'Will you stop swearing –'

'NO – NO – NO! the more you talk the more I'll swear.'

There was another battle in the mornings.

'Chloë get out of bed please, I've got to go and muck out.'

'I'm not stopping you.'

'You've got school!' I'd grab the duvet and she'd scream and kick.

'YAAAGOWAY! GET THE FUCK OFF AND LEAVE ME ALONE!'

If I asked her to tidy her room she'd rant and squeal.

'THIS HOUSE IS TOO SMALL, I'M CHOKING IN HERE, THERE'S NO ROOM!'

At breakfast she'd throw her spoon down. 'It's horrible! It tastes of METAL! I can't eat out of that filthy SPOON!'

Any time, she'd slide downstairs head first. Or sit for hours under the table, randomly yelling about dogshit, or shouting at me – 'I WISH YOU'D HAVE A HEART ATTACK AND DIE.'

As the spring nights lengthened I found her missing from her room several times. Our new land ran alongside a main road, and I found her riding my horse – just under seventeen hands, weight over six hundred kilos – around the field bareback in the dark. The first time I caught her she slid off and climbed up a tree and refused to come down. I took the horse back to the stable and sat with him, weeping. It happened again. I couldn't sleep. I was irritable with my owners and they moved their horses elsewhere. It would be months before I could restart the business.

She made a lot of noise in the house but the baby slept through most of it. The dogs curled closer. My stress level was permanently elevated.

+++

In October, we sat in front of the GP again. He read the teachers' emails I'd printed out. She'd thrown everything off her desk. She'd stormed out, shouting. She'd sworn at another kid. And at a teacher. She 'needs to play her part by arriving at all the lessons and causing less disruption' one email said. Voice of reason, I'd thought bitterly. You try it.

'They'll exclude her permanently. That's what I'm worried about.'

He said, 'What d'you think, Chloë? Has anybody at school suggested excluding you?'

'Dunno, don't care.' She was looking out of the window, vacantly. Somebody was parking a car.

He got up and went to the door. 'We'll take you for weighing and measuring and so on.'

The nurse came in and took her away. He went back to his desk.

I said 'I don't know what I'm doing wrong. It's confrontation, morning till night. Every time I ask her to do anything she shouts NO. I've tried smacking her, sending her to her room, grounding her, rewarding her, paying her .... nothing works. She says she hates me, she wishes I was dead, she wants to live with somebody else. Why does she hate me so much? And the foul language. Once I washed her mouth out with soap. My granny did that to me. But it's not that—'

'It's not you, Juliette. You brought up Joe, didn't you? And Gemma's the picture of health.' I'd run into him in the supermarket when I had the baby with me.

'Stop blaming yourself. I'm a clinician. We need a psychiatric diagnosis. I'll refer her to CAMHS again.'

'Cams?'

'Child and Adolescent Mental Health Services.'

'Oh, right.'

'Don't worry. Let me write it now, and you'll have a copy.'

We went home. Chloë was quiet in the car. I thought *Maybe I should just say yes all the time. Give her what she wants.* When she got out of the car I felt tears welling up. I was tired. I just wanted her to love me the way she had when she was little.

Later that week there was another stiff letter from the school. I asked her to read it. All about more swearing and shouting.

'That's a big fat lie,' she said. 'I never did any of that. They're always picking on me.'

I took her out before they excluded her, and got her into another school within days. She was a pretty girl with a mane of curly hair, the sort who's always popular. You'd think she was an angel until she opened her mouth, or got up and walked out, or tried to clamber downstairs head first. She started at the new place on the Monday after half term. On Thursday that week she came home crying. 'They're all horrible!'

Some girls in her class were being spiteful about her on Facebook and Snapchat. I went to the headmistress, who apologised and told them off. It kept on happening, though.

'I'm not GOING to school. I CAN'T GO! Why would you want me to go there and get bullied? They all gang up! They're horrible to me! Don't you understand?'

I had another meeting with the the headmistress – and another NHS letter saying that the GP's referral would not be taken up 'on this occasion'. Christ, on what occasion would it? Chloë went back to school.

A couple of nights later, after eleven o'clock, I switched off all the lights downstairs and went up to bed. I was pulling my bedroom curtains when I saw a blue light flashing through the trees. A police car turned into the drive and two uniformed officers started to get out.

I ran downstairs and opened the door.

'Hallo?'

'Do you have a Chloë Mare here?' the woman asked me.

'Yes, she's my daughter. Is something wrong? She's in her room, she's asleep.'

'Would you mind checking to see if she's okay? Just call her down, would you?'

I went to the bottom of the stairs.

'Chloë!'

A pause. 'What?'

'Come down here, please.' I turned to the police, my mind racing. *Shoplifting? Had she attacked somebody?*

'What's going on?'

'We've been asked to see her,' the man said quietly. 'Don't worry.'

They came in. Leaves swirled into the hall with them; it was a cold November night. The man took off his peaked hat, and they stood in the living room.

Chloë came to the doorway in her pyjamas, looking scared.

'Chloë Mare?'

'Yes.'

'You called Childline an hour ago.'

'So what?'

'You remember what you said?'

'Yes, but that's private.'

'Not if you threaten suicide, love.'

I couldn't believe this. '*WHAT?*'

The woman murmured, 'Chloë was talking about hanging herself.'

I sat down. My knees felt like jelly. I was horrified.

'I didn't *mean* it,' Chloë said. 'It was a joke.'

'Well, what did you think would happen, Chloë? The lady who took your call was very upset. That's why we're here.'

'I didn't know she'd call you. I didn't know it was a real person.'

They were very nice, the police. They took some details and gave her a gentle warning and after they'd gone she went to bed. So did I. I couldn't quite believe what I'd heard. I curled up shivering and thinking of all the terrible things you see on TV. Self-harm, a spate of teenage suicides in the Welsh valleys... I didn't want to let her out of my sight ever again.

What do you say, what do you do, what do you think? Next morning I woke up in a state of dread. *Chloë had called Childline and talked about hanging herself.* I was close to tears. I didn't take her to school. I wanted help. The GP had already been turned down twice. I would have to push until I got somewhere. I didn't know who else to call so I rang Child Welfare at the council.

I poured out my troubles, in tears some of the time, to a Welfare Officer.

'I'm desperate. I've never been in this situation before. She wasn't joking. It was a cry for help. You *have* to do something *please*. I'm not going to see my child on TV dead 'cos no one would do anything.'

I don't think he knew what to say.

'I'd advise you to call Pelston if you're worried. Ask about getting her sectioned.'

Pelston Grange was the nearest mental hospital. I thought that was a bit extreme, a 28-day section (detention in hospital) – I didn't even know if you could section a child of thirteen. But Chloë must be desperate to talk about hanging. I didn't make that call; I just took her out of the school.

For the third time, the GP – exasperated – wrote to CAMHS. Life seemed to be on hold until we got that appointment. They had always taken ages to write back and I wanted help now.

I didn't want to trouble my mother. Her partner was seriously ill and she was recovering from surgery herself. But I had nobody else and I knew she worried about Chloë. I felt completely out of my depth and I could trust her. She agreed to go halves on a diagnosis from a Harley Street psychiatric clinic. It would cost £900 for an initial report but I'd researched ADHD on the internet and I knew a paediatrician alone couldn't help.

London was two hours away. I told the receptionist this was an emergency but the earliest appointment they could offer was at eight a.m. on Christmas Eve, three weeks away. I didn't hesitate. Afterwards I wondered how I'd ever get her there but the appointment was a beacon of certainty shining through hopeless gloom and I went for it. I now had a backstop, in case CAMHS refused for a third time. I was willing to sell everything I had to pay for some answers.

+++

I got Chloë into yet another school. She seemed to be settling in but then she usually did, at first. At home by myself, with Gemma asleep in her cot in the afternoons, my anxiety hit new heights. I started searching Chloë's bedroom. I was looking for clues, I suppose; something to help me understand why she'd made that call. Nothing. I looked on the internet, not knowing if what I found was an answer, or just a futile exercise that ratcheted up the worry.

After days of this I called CAMHS. A young woman answered. I told her whose mother I was and when the GP's letter had been sent. She asked me to hold on for a minute.

'Oh yes, they've got it,' she said. 'It was logged last Wednesday.'

'Well, have they made a decision?'

'You'll get a letter. It's usually seven to ten days.'

'That's not good enough. I need to know now.'

'I'm afraid I can't help. The team make the decision—'

'My daughter's thirteen and she's threatened to kill herself! This is an emergency!' I heard my voice rising. 'Who's the manager there? I want their email address.'

'Er – okay. Wait a minute, please.'

After a long pause she came back and gave me the woman's details. I dashed off a furious email headed CHLOË MARE REFERRAL; I gave her date of birth.

I went to my GP on two occasions months ago about my daughter and someone not clinically qualified decided twice that she didn't need to see a psychiatrist. **My daughter wants to hang herself.** *CAMHS is not willing to see reports about her problems. I think it's disgusting that I cannot get trained help for her. Unless*

I get the appointment that my GP, who is qualified and has seen her, has requested then I will take this further.

I knew that putting this on record meant it would be logged and someone would read it. If anything happened to Chloë now, the manager would know there was an email trail that could lead to a charge of negligence at the very least.

Two days later, they notified me of Chloë's appointment with an MHP (mental health practitioner) on 14th December. They gave me a number to call in case of emergency. I cancelled Harley Street.

+++

We had twelve days to wait. Leading up to that meeting, life at home got worse. She wouldn't go on the bus to school. I had to drive her. I would be bombarded with forty or fifty text messages a day reminding me to pick her up on time. She wouldn't eat anything with flour in it, and the next day she only wanted fruit. She was hoarding used paper cups and other rubbish. She obsessively turned switches off. She blamed me, swore at me, when Gemma cried or the dogs barked. She'd deliberately run up and down the stairs while I was trying to carry the baby up. She sat under the dining table for hours on end.

I didn't know why this was happening. I just wanted her to be well again. I gave up being patient – which didn't work – and I'd shout back, argue with her, pull her out from under the table. I told her my phone was broken so that she wouldn't bombard me with messages from the minute she arrived at school. And every day now I searched her bedroom. There was never any clue to her uncontrollable anger. Just chocolate wrappings, empty plastic bottles, unwashed plates and glasses, used sanitary towels, underwear that hadn't been washed for days. When I confronted her with this evidence of poor personal hygiene she shouted, picked up a cup and threw it at me, and snatched a sharp knife out of the kitchen drawer and threatened to stab me. The baby was crying, the dogs were barking – it was hell.

I quit. I left her alone for twenty minutes, saying I was going to the shop in the village. I just needed to get away. I parked the car in a layby and cried. I was desperate. I rang the emergency number I'd been given.

'I feel like driving into a tree and killing myself.'

A man and woman turned up within fifteen minutes in an estate car marked 'ambulance service'. They were kind; sat in my car and talked me down. They drove home with me. Chloë had shut herself into her room. They sat in the living room and listened to me while I tried to describe my dread of getting through even another week of this. Trying to calm me down, the man suggested I get a pet for her, something she could look after herself.

'We've already got three dogs, four cats and a hamster. She's not particularly interested.'

'Well something she can love and call her own, something she's responsible for – a rabbit would be good. Rabbits come out to play at dusk and dawn, so it'd keep her busy after school. Try it – let us know how it goes.'

I'd do anything to stop her shouting abuse at me. The next morning I drove to a big pet shop and bought a perky-looking grey rabbit, a roomy cage, a litterbox, hay, special food, everything. The whole lot was installed in her room. For a few days everything went according to plan: she spent most of her time up there, playing with the rabbit. But she refused to clean his tray and when I did it, she shouted at me for going in when she wasn't there. The room began to smell. One evening I went to the bottom of the stairs. Her door was ajar.

'Chloë!'

'WHAT?'

'There's a terrible smell all the time. Smokey needs to live down here where I can clean his cage and feed him along with the others.'

'NO! He's MY RABBIT. You don't know anything. NO!'

'I know he needs a clean litterbox. I can smell it from here. That's unkind. He'll get sick and so will you. Listen, you can keep him up there at weekends – what are you—?'

She'd flung her door wide and hurled the whole cage at me. The bedding and litter and food and water went all over the walls and the floor and me. The cage lay on its side. I ran upstairs, grabbed Smokey, and left her. She was screaming with rage and pulling bedclothes off the bed, pictures off the wall, and drawers out of a cupboard. I shut her in, calmed the terrified rabbit and took him back to the shop the next day.

I didn't think of myself as someone who needed to keep calling social workers or whoever they were but I knew I couldn't cope on my own; my daughter was getting dangerous, and my mother was as worried as I was. So I rang the emergency number again when Chloë was at school. I was embarrassed by feeling so so helpless, but I told them what had happened. They were very good, and promised to send a couple of senior mental health workers to help me when Chloë got home. 'They're an Intensive Support Team,' the woman explained, in a comfortable sort of way. 'They always come in when there's a crisis so they're used to dealing with situations like this. They'll kind of work out what's going on and what needs doing.'

Two cheerful women came to the door. At first Chloë refused to come downstairs, so I sat and talked to them, but after five minutes she wanted to see what was going on. She came hopping into the room making loud EE-AW noises like a donkey.

'Chloë shut UP!'

'EEe-AW!' She flopped to the floor and started wriggling across the carpet like a demented snake.

'HEY,' said one of them. 'Chloë!'

'FUCK OFF you fat cow –'

'CHLOË!'

'We'd like you to sit down so that we can talk. Will you do that?'

She jumped up and ran to the cupboard under the stairs and shut herself in, holding onto the handle inside. They tried to talk to her from the hall but all she did was swear.

'Listen to us, Chloë. Your mum wants—'

'Why should I CARE what my mum wants? My mum talks a heap of SHIT. There's nothing wrong with me.'

She barged out and pushed past them and up the stairs and slammed into her room.

I don't know why, probably because these women were so nice and looked so sorry for me, but I burst into tears.

'Juliette, you will get through this. She very probably does have ADHD and some other issues as well but you won't know until you see the MHP on Monday. But whatever it is, there will be treatment and it will help.'

'What kind of treatment?'

'There is medication for ADHD, but don't quote me on that because we don't yet know if that's what it is. It may be more complex. Wait until you've seen the mental health practitioner. In the meantime you need some support. We'll get somebody out to you as a matter of urgency.'

I was on the internet until about two in the morning, looking up ADHD. Wikipedia came up first. *Mental disorder of the neurodevelopmental type... characterized by problems paying attention, excessive activity, or difficulty controlling behavior which is not appropriate for a person's age. These symptoms begin by age six to twelve, are present for more than six*

*months, and cause problems in at least two settings
(such as school, home, or recreational activities).*

My blood ran cold. Chloë was a textbook case.

*30–50% of people diagnosed in childhood continue
to have symptoms into adulthood.*

This wasn't going away. I was panicking. I rang
my son. He laughed.

'Mum, calm down. She can be a pain; it's just the
way she is. All she needs is a smack.'

I rang my brother. 'Get a grip, Juliette. That girl
just knows how to wind you up. Stop spoiling her!
She'll grow out of it as soon as you stop giving her
everything she wants.'

Only my mother said she'd always thought
something was wrong with Chloë. She started doing
her own research. And December 14th arrived at last.

+++

The mental health practitioner was an hour's drive
away. Chloë sat still and said hardly a word on the
way there: a first. Somehow she knew this was

serious. I was just glad that at last I'd be heard by somebody who would understand and we'd get help.

The address turned out to be an innocuous-looking modern house with trees around and parking for about five cars in front. A brass plate next to the front door announced CAMHS. There was an entryphone and we were buzzed in to a small lobby. There was a toughened-glass door in front of us when we got in, and a security officer came out from behind a desk to open it. I looked up and saw a camera. A smiling woman in glasses emerged from a door at the side.

'Hi, Juliette. Hallo, Chloë. I'm your MHP.' She told me her name but I immediately forgot it. Getting into the building was not straightforward. She checked the time and signed us in at the desk. Laminate floors, soundproofing, security, furniture screwed down... this place was set up to protect staff who might have to deal with violent outbursts.

The MHP opened another lobby door with her card and took us into a large consulting room. There were armchairs for us and she sat at a desk so that she could make notes on her computer. She asked for a bit of background about the family from me, and then turned to Chloë.

'Tell me about a typical day,' she said. 'Not today necessarily, but most days. How does it begin?'

Chloë had no trouble talking. She told the MHP how she got up at five a.m. every day and at five past five she would unplug her phone from the charger and go back to bed and play games on it until six a.m. She then put her television on to watch a certain programme for forty minutes. At twenty to seven exactly she would lay out her clothes for school, which took five minutes. At six forty-five a.m. she would have a shower.

The MHP was tapping all this into the computer.

'I didn't know any of that,' I said, astonished.

'No.'

'You certainly like rules and boundaries, Chloë. What about making your bed and so on? Have you got a routine for that?'

'No. Making beds and tidying are pointless. They always need doing again so you might as well not bother. I hate doing that.'

'What other things d'you hate?'

'NOISE. Gemma's always YELLING. It drives me crazy. And the dogs YAP AND YAP but Mum never shuts them up when I tell her to.'

'Do they make a noise in the mornings?'

'Not specially. They keep quiet when I get my breakfast. That's at seven forty-five.'

'What d'you have for breakfast?'

'Well if there's a tin of fruit cocktail I have that. But it's got to say FRUIT COCKTAIL on the tin. If it says Fruit Salad I don't like it. And I only have yoghurt at weekends. I have Chocolate Corner. Always.'

'What's wrong with other kinds?'

'I don't like them. I don't like Greek or fruit or anything. I only like Chocolate Corner.'

'Anything to add, Juliette?'

'Some of this is news to me. I'm not around on weekdays before eight,' I told the woman. 'I stay upstairs till it's time to take Chloë to school.'

'Any particular reason?'

Tears came to my eyes. 'The nastiness. I just can't face the arguments.'

'Oh stop fucking BLUBBING, Mum! You're really *irritating.*'

We were there for three hours and the MHP took a lot of notes. She heard about violence, Chloë's habit of talking so fast that she couldn't be understood, hoarding, Chloë talking in her sleep a lot. At the end she said, 'I think there's cause for concern here, and I'm going to refer Chloë for psychiatric assessment so you can expect a letter. The appointment will be after Christmas now. There will be a diagnosis possibly featuring ADHD and – or – an autism spectrum disorder. And ultimately treatment.'

Huge relief washed over me, although I was wondering how to get through Christmas. She added, 'Can I confirm that I have your consent to discuss what I've heard with colleagues? Because I want to make sure you always have someone to turn to, and the Intensive Support Team need to be involved as soon as possible.'

'Yes, okay.'

'You'll be hearing from them very soon.'

I did. Two IST workers turned up the very next day when Chloë was at school. Judy, a mixed-race woman carrying a floppy leather bag full of paperwork, was for me to talk to, and Simon, who was much younger, long-haired and from Belfast, was going to work with my daughter to keep her calm. I was glad of the offer but wary.

I said, 'Look, please don't be offended but I have followed a lot of false trails already. I've called people from every charity and social agency I could google, and they've all sympathised and given me lots of advice. I've had advice up to here, but half these people don't know anything about what it's really like to live with a child like Chloë. It's taken more than a year even to see the MHP. How much experience have you got, really? Because I need proper help from specialists with professional experience.'

Judy said, 'Of course you do. That's fine. I've worked with ADHD kids in a special school since 1995. I still do, two days a week.'

'I work there too,' Simon said. 'I've qualified more recently so to some extent I'm still learning.'

'But you can handle a kid in a rage.'

'Yes. I've been trained to do that.'

I stayed wary for a while. But they were nearly always available when I needed them and gradually I got to trust both of them. Chloë met Simon and somehow he developed a rapport with her. He was there when she rang him. Sometimes I told her to talk to him when something made her angry. Other times she rang just because she wanted somebody to confide in other than me.

Judy became my rock. I was entirely sceptical at first. I didn't believe she'd be any more competent than any other well-meaning advisor. She needed to prove to me she knew what she was talking about. This she did, and after a few meetings and phone calls she could explain all the weird things my daughter did and why she did them. I was learning the jargon. If she yelled NO! and threw something, this was 'exhibiting oppositional behaviour'. If she insisted on one set of routines, it was 'rigidity'. Judy would ask me questions like...Does she flap her hands? Does she speak very fast? Does she interrupt when you're talking? Does she shout? Does she take risks, physically? Does she make up rules and regs?

Chloë came up with most of these attitudes and behaviours some of the time. Judy explained that for various reasons, mostly because of anxiety and an imperative desire for control, these behaviours were typical of people who had ADHD or were on the autism spectrum.

'What's that? I thought autistic people didn't communicate much at all.'

'Some don't. It's difficult to explain but autism varies so much between individuals that in order to make a diagnosis we kind of score people against known symptoms. And there's an overlap between autism and ADHD, just as there's an overlap between ADHD and occasionally behaving like a spoiled brat. Don't worry; you'll get help from the psychiatrist.'

Finally someone could see how hard this was for me. Judy could tell me how to avoid making Chloë kick off and what to do if she did, but I couldn't change my own patterns easily. Chloë instinctively knew what buttons to press to get the one reaction that would escalate things. Simon seemed able to calm her down but I had only to answer her and I'd pour fuel on the fire. I started asking how to avoid making her worse. What do I do? How do I calm her down? How do I make her not so paranoid? – impulsive? – loud? – rude? – mean? – violent? It was hard to learn.

I had so many questions and only an hour. Judy was the only person who could help me, right now, understand my child.

'What d'you think the psychiatrist will say?'

'I'm not in a position to know. If it is ADHD, it's usually medication.'

'Does it work? I don't like the idea of giving drugs to a child.'

'Nobody does. But, in my experience, yes. It works. It's transformative, eventually. It's never easy to get the dosage right though. It's trial and error.'

I wished I'd known years ago that medication could take this suffering away. I thought of the years I'd wasted when different primary schools kept telling me something was wrong and I'd been in denial. It had taken a call to Childline to jerk me into certainty that she needed help.

So did I. I wanted my cuddly, loving child back.
The psychiatrist's appointment in January, and the
possibility of a change in Chloë, kept me going.

+++

Joe was home for Christmas. We hadn't seen him
since October and I felt better with him around. Even
if he did think I was exaggerating everything and all
his half-sister needed was a smack.

As it turned out Christmas Day, dark and wet out
in the fields, was awful. With presents strewn around
her, Chloë talked obsessively all morning about Hitler
and the Holocaust. Could it get worse? Not a lot, but
she could find a way. Over Christmas dinner she
decided to impart all the swear-words she knew in
different languages, with translations. She
exasperated Harry, my normally even-tempered
brother, to such a point of fury that he stood up and
sent her to her room.

We all had peace and quiet with no interruptions
for a good half hour, and time to talk about cheerful
things and make a fuss of the baby. Then Harry called
her down. No answer. He went upstairs. Joe had gone

out with the dogs in pouring rain and I was in the kitchen loading the dishwasher. Harry came in.

'Where is she? She's not in her room. I've looked everywhere.'

The two of us spent forty minutes calling her, opening cupboards, looking under beds, checking outbuildings in the wet, and generally wasting our time and searching the same places over and over, with help from Joe when he came back. I was desperately anxious, trying to stop thinking about that call to Childline. My brother, who blamed himself, put his coat on and got his car keys; he thought she must have walked down to the village and was going out to look. I was about to call the police when Joe shouted loudly from upstairs

'She's here!'

He'd pulled clothes out of a half-open drawer in her room and found her hiding underneath.

We were more relieved than anything. We talked. We played games. We watched telly, drank wine and ate cake. We did the stuff people do. Chloë was loud, but not unbearable. Then she said, out of the blue

'I want to call my Dad.'

'Who?' Joe said, startled. My brother rolled his eyes at the ceiling.

'My Dad. I want to call him.'

'No, you don't,' Joe said quickly. 'You really don't.' He was six years older and had been eight when I threw Chloë's father out for the very last time. Joe had vivid memories of the nasty piece of work he'd been.

'I've got a right to see my own father if I want.'

'Look, Mum's got other things to think about, so drop it.'

I told her, 'I'm not going to contact him now, even if I can find him, because after Christmas we have an important appointment. We've to get that out of the way. And I'm going to take advice on whether it's a good idea anyway, so don't start going on about it.'

'But I WANT—'

'That's enough! Just shut up for once, Chloë,' Joe said. And she did. For a while.

+++

2016

The appointment with the psychiatrist was at the beginning of January. In the days leading up to it, Chloë got worse. She played roughly with Gemma, throwing her into the air and swinging her round by her arms. I started carrying Gemma around the house, never letting her out of my sight, but in an unguarded minute I caught Chloë throwing her about again. I made her stop. She stared at me.

'Why?'

'Because she's only thirteen months old. She's fragile. You could hurt her badly, so *don't do that again*!'

'What if I sat on her, would she die? Would I get into trouble?'

I snatched Gemma off the floor. 'I'd throw you out the house before you got anywhere near her.' Chloë tried to pull the baby away from me.

'STOP IT, CHLOË! Don't you dare touch her.'

I was scared of her now. The next day Gemma was in day-care while I looked after my horse, as usual, and when I brought her back I warned Chloë not to touch her. Chloë was frightened and angry and I was, too. I came close to hating her. I called the MHP and told her what was going on.

She said, 'You're doing the right thing. Keep the baby away from her. Listen, I'm sorry about this, Juliette, but I'm going to have to report the situation to Social Care.'

'What?'

'Well, Gemma's in danger, isn't she? I have to make a report in writing – that's the procedure. I'd be professionally negligent if I didn't. They're responsible for the health and welfare of children at risk. This is something they have to deal with. '

'What'll they do?'

'I'm sure it'll be fine, don't worry. They'll probably visit and offer you whatever support they can and the problem will go away. Let me know if you need help.'

Next day I decided to put Gemma into the nursery for longer, for her safety. If I picked her up at five p.m., she would only be up for an hour before bed time and I could supervise her the whole time.

A woman who said she was 'Pauline Race from the Social Care Team' left her name and number in a voicemail. 'This is for Miss Mare. I'll be making a home visit to you when both children are at home. I'm looking at tomorrow afternoon. Please will you confirm.'

My blood ran cold. She sounded bossy. These people could take children away. I didn't see what could possibly qualify her to come in and pass judgement without knowing anything about us. I hadn't done anything wrong. I called her back and said, 'That's not convenient. I've got a lot on tomorrow and Gemma will be in the nursery all day.'

'Well, I'm afraid you'll have to change those arrangements. You need to make sure both children are at the house.'

We started to argue. We compromised. She'd visit us after the meeting with the psychiatrist. After that call I wished I'd never told the MHP about the baby. I should have just dealt with it. This Social Care woman didn't know how strong I was. I would never let anything happen to Gemma.

Judy wanted to come to our meeting with Dr Salt, the psychiatrist.

'Oh no, it's okay. You don't need to be there.' For me, the meeting was private. I wanted to be first to hear and understand what was wrong with my daughter. *Does she think I'm not strong enough or bright enough or something?* She read my mind.

'Juliette, don't worry, I won't take over or anything. But if you have a professional with you who's witnessed Chloë's behaviour at first hand, it strengthens your case. I can reassure her that you're not exaggerating. I've seen how bad things can get for you and what hard work Chloë can be.'

I saw the point of that. I wasn't going to leave that meeting with my daughter unless I had some medication for her, and I might need backup.

I drove to another CAMHS office, not much different from the first one, but in the grounds of a hospital and over the border in another county. Judy was there waiting for us.

Dr Salt was a small, dark woman. She sat at her desk, next to her laptop, and saw us settled into chairs. She had a notepad in front of her.

'Okay. We have two hours together, and I hope we end up with a diagnosis by the end of this meeting, so I'm going to start with the list of presenting complaints. Let me know if you disagree with any of these... Shouting, making physical threats towards Mum, obsessive texting, excessive dependency, obsessional behaviour, hiding, threatening to run away, sensory issues, hyperactivity, rigidity....' I was nodding as the list went on.

'Chloë, d'you have anything to say about that?' Dr Salt asked at the end.

Chloë had been squirming on her chair, or swinging her legs. Now she said nothing but slid onto the floor.

'All right. So we'll revisit some of this to clarify it. Juliette, when did the shouting start?'

'She's always shouted. Even when she was little.'

'How were you physically threatened?'

I explained about the knife and the threats to push me downstairs, which had started since Christmas, and the way Chloë gripped my wrists tightly when she got angry.

'What about all these texts, Chloë? Why d'you text your mum so much?'

'She might forget to pick me up from school if I didn't.' She was back on the chair now, but fidgeting all the time.

'What's the worst thing that could happen then?'

'I'd have to walk home and it's a main road.'

'Has that ever happened?'

'Once she was late and I wanted to go to the toilet.'

'When was that?'

'Year six.'

I said, 'She always wants to know where I am and what I'm doing. She's always been like that. What time will you be back, how long will it take... It's constant, since she was little, like she needs to control me.

Sometimes you just lie on the sofa and cling to me, don't you?' Chloë shrugged.

'Why d'you worry about your mum, Chloë?'

She didn't know.

I said, 'When she was about four, my son's father beat me up and Chloë saw it. She was afraid of men for a while after that.'

Gradually we worked through the list. 'Sensory issues' included more than hating loud noise; touch and taste were issues too. Chloë could not tolerate cold food or cold drinks or scratchy clothes. 'Rigidity' meant she would fly into a rage if somebody was late for an appointment or I didn't have exactly the right food in the house. Also, the rigidity with which she stuck to her own routines. We discussed poor concentration, hyperactivity, animal noises, swearing, shouting at teachers (who Chloë said were lying), getting up and walking about in class, riding in the dark, and so on and so on... Right now, in the shortest days of January, Chloë insisted on arriving home before dusk. I had to park up before we got to the house to get the horses in from the paddocks, which meant leaving Gemma with Chloë in the car for up to fifteen minutes; and if Gemma started to cry, Chloë would get agitated, and I'd have to run over and ... horses, baby, Chloë, I had to sort them all out at once.

I was living in a dictatorship run by a girl of thirteen.

'D'you watch TV?' Dr Salt asked her.

'Yes.'

'If something sad happens to people, do you feel sad?'

'No. It's not real.'

'What about your mum, when she gets upset, d'you feel sad then?'

'No. She gets over it.'

On the plus side, she could spend hours alone playing a game or doing a puzzle and she could clean stables to perfection; she was fussy about exactly which hook each piece of tack was hung on and what colour blanket my horse must wear, and at weekends, and in school holidays, she would get up early and clean all four stables meticulously.

Judy added a lot about Chloë's anxiety and her kicking me and her generally over-controlling behaviour. I'd shown her a list of commands Chloë had written for me, and she asked me to show it to Dr Salt. I had a copy on my phone.

RULES

Use my things correctly and treat both my TV and my remote control with a great portion of respect.

Clean regularly.

Keep out of reach of children (meaning Gemma).

Do not throw, drop, man-handle or even mess with my remote control.

Both TV and remote are in perfection mode at the minute, and I would like them to stay in good condition throughout the time of using 'my' property.

Carefully place control down onto a sturdy surface 2 metres from ground.

Turn off all devices after each and every use.

DO NOT THROW PAPER AWAY.

If you disagree with my rules and regulations please list, below, correct information. Name, date, signature, time.

Thanks for reading this.

Good luck and don't break the law.

Much appreciation.

Chloë Mare

(£2.50 FINE IF NOT FOLLOWED.)

After almost two hours, in danger of over-running into the next patient's time, we got winding-up signals: the conclusion. Some of Chloë's symptoms were consistent with ADHD but others, like the aggression and over-attachment, might indicate anxiety which resulted in controlling behaviour so she was probably on the autistic spectrum; and she might have learning difficulties... Dr Salt thought talking therapy would help, and family therapy...

'So – I will be writing to you. It's been good to meet—'

'I understand there's medication,' I interrupted. She looked shocked.

'In the long term...'

'She's completely unmanageable after school. She screams, she bangs about, she doesn't calm down until about seven o'clock and I can't cope, Doctor. I've got the baby, I've got work... '

'Yes I appreciate that, but—'

'I'm *not taking her home without a prescription* to control the way she is. If I don't get that, I'll leave her right here.'

Dr Salt looked startled at this sudden assertiveness. Judy said, 'I can back Juliette up. I've seen how hard it is.'

'Well,' Dr Salt said. 'Okay. So – one condition at a time. I can prescribe methylphenidate for the ADHD. You've probably heard it called Ritalin – it's the same thing. But we have to start with a low dose. Five milligrams after breakfast and five milligrams at four p.m. for two weeks and then we'll review. You see Chloë twice a week, Judy, so could you monitor progress for us?'

It wouldn't be a miracle cure but it was a start. Dr Salt said something about assessments and Connors (a Behaviour Rating Scale used by teachers, but I didn't know that) and questionnaires – SCQs – and the ADOS assessment team... and an OT for the sensory issues... I sat in a swirling fog of acronyms I didn't understand, but hanging onto the big news: Chloë would be medicated for ADHD and she was going to be assessed for some kind of autism as well.

I'd pushed and I'd pushed and I'd got action at last. Drugs! Yay, bring 'em on. Getting a diagnosis and a prescription was my first victory in more than a year of trying.

Dr Salt warned me the process would be long, and getting the dosage right would take time, and on our way out Judy said, 'You'll be up against different challenges...' I listened to both of them, without understanding or really believing most of what they said; I was just relieved. We left, having over-run into the next person's appointment, and I picked up the prescription at the hospital's dispensary on the way out.

Hold on, Juliette. Nothing's that easy. We'd set off for home when Chloë, in the back seat, said, 'What was all that about? There's nothing wrong with me. I'm not taking pills.'

'There is, and you'll have to.'

'I'm not going to take them.'

'Yes, you are.'

'Well I won't. I TOLD YOU.'

She'd started kicking my back through the seat. We were still only a mile from the clinic, in light, fast traffic on a bypass between ploughed fields. I thought *Jesus, she's going to keep on like this all the way home.* I took a deep breath and considered my response.

When the kicking stopped I said, 'What's the worst that can happen if you do take the medication?'

'I don't know.'

'What's the worst that can happen if you don't?'

'Who fucking CARES?'

'I do. Because unless something happens, the rate you're going, there could be consequences –'

'What consequences?'

'I don't know. I'm telling you, Chloë, you're now in a *system*. The system records that *you need to take medication*. If—'

The world went black.

A fraction of a second at sixty miles an hour. My hand flew to my face and I ripped her coat off it. *We haven't hit anything the car in front is still there I have to pull over –*

Autopilot. I found myself pulling up in a small car park in front of the one house along this whole road: a Chinese restaurant on a left-hand turn. My heart was pounding. I was shaking. I didn't turn round. I leaned on the steering wheel and yelled furiously at her image in the rear-view mirror.

'YOU IDIOT WHAT DID YOU DO THAT FOR YOU STUPID *STUPID* GIRL WE COULD BOTH HAVE BEEN KILLED DON'T YOU KNOW ANYTHING?'

I was trembling all over. I got out of the car, locked her in and walked round and round the car park until I felt calm enough to drive.

+++

I drove on in silence. Close to home she said

'Okay. I promise I'll be good. Now I won't have to take the pills, will I?'

I couldn't answer. I couldn't take even one more negative. I knew I would have to bribe her, so I stopped at Tesco before we got home and got a variety-pack of sweets. When she'd taken her pill she could choose one. There was a lot of moaning and 'Aagh! it's stuck in my throat' coughing, but I got it down her.

She took her pill for the next few days. Then out of the blue came blank refusal. Physical struggle. Force. I dragged her into the kitchen and *made* her take it. I couldn't believe I'd done that. This mustn't go on.

Pauline Race, the Social Care worker, turned up around then, late one schoolday afternoon. I'd told Chloë that somebody was coming to check that she was safe to be around Gemma.

'What d'you mean safe?'

'Gentle, I mean. This social worker wants to be sure you won't ever frighten the baby. So you'd better behave. I don't want you to to touch Gemma or talk about her and if you feel in any way bothered by that, just go to your room.'

'Whatever.'

At four o'clock that afternoon I opened the cupboard.

'Chloë, where are your pills?'

'Dunno.'

The doorbell rang. Pauline Race was a tall disapproving-looking blonde woman carrying what I came to recognise as the typical social worker's handbag-and-briefcase combo. I had to explain what was going on. I couldn't sit down and talk until I'd given my daughter her tablets, which....

So we spent the first half hour looking for them. And when I found them, it was another fifteen minutes before she would take her pill. I felt mortified. I showed this woman the letter from Dr Salt with the ADHD diagnosis and explained that the medication would control Chloë's behaviour. She said nothing. I don't think she knew anything about mental health. But surely she could see this situation was not of my making. I thought the paperwork saying Chloë was being treated would put her mind at rest.

Two days later I got a letter from her. I was to attend a CIN (Child in Need) meeting at Chloë's school in three weeks' time. I called the CAMHS office number on the letter. Pauline Race wasn't in, so I spoke to somebody else. I explained the situation in detail.

'What's a Child in Need meeting?'

The woman had a flat irritating voice and a verbal tic.

'Oh, your daughter doesn't go, obviously. It's about welfare. The social care team and professionals and carers have a meeting, obviously, to decide whether the domestic environment is appropriate. If abuse seems to be going on, then obviously they can remove the baby to a place of safety. Or if a minor is dangerous to others he or she can be removed, obviously.'

Obviously. This was surreal. It couldn't be happening. One or both of my daughters could be taken away.

I had to do something. I spoke to the owner of the nursery where Gemma was. I asked if my baby was happy. Did she cry more than usual? Had they noticed any change in her personality? They hadn't, but were worried about why I was asking. Reluctantly, I told them about her sister's diagnosis and the visit from Social Care and the meeting which was supposed to confirm that Gemma hadn't been mishandled in any way by her sister. There was no shame in what I revealed – after all, it was nobody's fault that Chloë had this condition – but I felt shame. It felt like confessing that we'd been identified as a problem family.

+++

By the day of the Child In Need meeting in February Dr Salt had got us onto waiting lists for one-to one-therapy and had asked the GP to organise a specialist occupational therapist to help with Chloë's sensory issues. She'd also asked Chloë's former school for an assessment and her current school for a 'common assessment framework' and an educational psychology assessment. I concluded that a lot of well-meaning attention was being paid, and I was pleased.

Also, she'd increased Chloë's medication, after explaining that there could be side-effects. My daughter was now on 10mg of methylphenidate twice a day instead of 5mg. Very slowly she was getting less excitable.

The other event in her life had been meeting her father, at the end of January. She'd demanded that every day since Christmas, so I tracked him down for her. I worried, though. I had no idea what effect this would have. He was obsessional himself.

In the event, they'd met in a MacDonalds near to where he lived and had very little to say to each other. She lost interest in him as soon as she'd met him, and when he found out she'd been diagnosed with a mental health problem, he melted out of her life like snow in a heatwave. I got one bullying email from him saying doctors over-medicate as a matter of course and his daughter shouldn't be taking drugs at her age. I didn't reply and I heard nothing more. Result.

Eight people altogether were at the Child in Need meeting. Pauline Race, the social worker who had visited just once, presided over it. Chloë's school nurse was there, as were a health visitor, a senior

mental health worker, two teachers from the school
and the owner of Gemma's nursery. I, as the parent,
was the minority of one who actually knew what
Chloë was like around the baby. All of us had to decide
whether Chloë was likely to harm Gemma. There was
a scored assessment, and a satisfactory outcome; a
care plan was put in place. In other words, everybody
there would play their part in keeping an eye on our
situation.

It was a good thing they weren't keeping an eye
the following afternoon. Judy was in the house with
me, and Simon was out with Chloë. He usually took
her into the village for a cup of coffee to give me a
break. A friend called me.

'Juliette – I just came in and and I wondered if you
knew there's a young guy with long hair riding
Harvey in the top field.'

'WHAT?'

Harvey is my horse. I was on my feet and heading
for the door already.

'Calm down. Chloë's with him.'

'For god's sake – PLEASE GET HIM OFF THE HORSE!'

I just ran. Paula Radcliffe couldn't have crossed that paddock faster than I did. Simon had never been on a horse in his life. He'd told me that. My horse, a highly bred showjumper with a sensitive mouth and hair-trigger responses, could throw him to the ground and break his neck, tear off with him if a crisp packet bowled across their path – every scenario possible flashed through my mind.

Thank god – ahead I saw the horse, placidly allowing my friend to walk him back to the stable. When I got to her she said, 'Who is that guy? He seemed clueless.'

'A total bloody idiot.'

'He said Chloë asked him to sit on the horse so he did.'

I was furious, trying to get my breath back. 'He's supposed to be looking after her! WHAT WAS HE THINKING?'

He apologised, but I never trusted him again. Chloë just laughed. I couldn't have her in the stables any more. The danger of putting an untrained rider on a big unpredictable animal did not bear thinking about. She had no idea of risk. She'd got Simon onto the horse because she could. When I saw Dr Salt we talked about impulsivity. She said, 'I'm cautious about increasing the medication, because beyond a certain level the side-effects can start to show. Volatility, sensory sensitivity to noise and so on. That doesn't mean that even higher doses won't calm those side-effects down. Prescribing for these conditions is very difficult indeed.'

She raised the dose to 27 mg of Concerta, slow-release, to be taken at breakfast time. Judy and Simon turned up at our house twice a week. I could never get hold of Pauline Race, but then I didn't see how she could help anyway.

+++

Chloë seemed suddenly more anxious. She texted me from school several hundred times a day. Her speech was getting faster as though she was trying to get her words out in one breath. Noise at home – the baby crying, the dogs barking – made her scream with fury. I dreaded picking her up from the school. She was at her most impulsive, implacable and uncontrollable then. She'd start a loud abusive argument as soon as she got in the car. Usually I just said yes, no, or kept quiet. If I shouted back her feet would start drumming hard on the back of my seat, which really frightened me. And if I forgot to drive with all the doors locked she'd open hers, forcing me to slow down and pull over, and then run away leaving me on the road.

I ran after her but lost her. I couldn't just drive off, though God knows I felt like it. I had to call the police. She ran away from the car several times that January and February and when they found her, as they always did, and brought her back, they'd be polite but I read in their faces that they thought I was an incompetent parent. They were not trained to deal with ADHD children and her behaviour frustrated them. They pretty clearly thought, like my son, that Chloë was nothing more than a brat in a tantrum.

Driving with this craziness in the car was just too dangerous. I told Judy I couldn't do it any longer.

'I don't know what to do. A taxi every day is just too expensive and what would they do if she kicked off, anyway?'

'What about the bus?'

'She has to wait for it. If it doesn't come on time, to the minute, she'll panic. And she hates the noise. And they only come on the half hour and the one she'd have to get will be standing room only with people going to the station... crowds are not – It's just not an option.'

'Leave it with me. I'll see if we can sort something out.'

Judy knew the system. She asked Dr Salt to write to the school transport department at the council, so that they'd provide a special needs taxi to take her to school and back every day. It was a good idea but within ten days I got a letter of refusal. The school was a mile outside the designated zone; no taxi.

Dr Salt tried again. It might take a while to get an answer, though. Meanwhile, Chloë had missed school for a week. *Does she stay at home all day because I won't go in the car with her? Do I take my chances and drive her?* I chose the second option, keeping quiet, saying Yes and No in the right places, never asking questions, hoping that the medication would be bumped up after our next appointment. All the time wondering how on earth I might persuade her to get the bus.

People had often pointed out that my instinctive hair-trigger responses to her defiance were fuel on the fire. I knew I had to be more passive, less reactive, to pick my arguments. It was hard. It didn't always work, either. When it didn't, Judy'd be on the phone, calming me down, suggesting a plan for what we could do. That was good enough for me. I finally had someone who knew what I was going through and came up with constructive help.

She suggested I go to some meetings to meet other parents in my situation. She told me about charities that organised seminars, and schools where there were regular meetings for families... I shrank from all of it. I am just not a joiner-in. I am not that sort of person. Cosy commiseration sessions were exactly what I didn't want. I didn't see myself sharing this embarrassing experience of parenthood with strangers. I'd always been strong-minded, outgoing, in control, a businesswoman...I think I told Judy some of this.

But in the middle of explaining I suddenly saw that I was just clinging to my self-image as an excuse not to change, and I thought *Yeah. That was then. This is now. Chloë has taken your life over; get used to it.* And I didn't like to reject Judy's advice after all she'd done for me. So I cast negativity aside and went to one of these events anyway.

Success! You're thinking. Changed her life!

Nah. It was awful. It was called a 'panel discussion', and it took place in an overlit room in an annexe to a primary school. As soon as you walked in you got that bad-breath smell of children who eat too many sweets. On a trestle table stood a tea urn, milk, sugar, thirty thick white cups and saucers, and ten big paper plates with biscuits arranged on them. There were stackable chairs. And the people fitted all my prejudices about the kind of person who goes in for this stuff; there were about twelve of them, mostly women, dressed in M&S at its dullest. They all moved like old people, as if they had nothing better to do with their time. Why not? Maybe, I thought, their children were in institutions.

The people from the charity had no first-hand experience in dealing with ADHD kids. They sat in front of us on a raised platform and talked about 'aspects of care' and quoted from various writers on the subject. I was reminded of a trainee nurse who'd kept chirruping, as I went through the most painful final stage of labour 'You're doing really well Mrs Mare!' *What did she know?* She had no idea what this felt like. And how will people whose knowledge of ADHD is purely theoretical help me?

When that was over there was a spatter of applause, a scraping of chairs and a mini-stampede for the tea and digestives.

I drove home. I knew what Judy had been getting at. I'd lost a lot of friends because of Chloë. She had insulted several of them. ('You've got baggy tits. Why don't you wear a bra?'– that sort of thing.) She'd had screaming fits once too often when they came round. And I can't even begin to explain how embarrassing it is to be overheard discussing somebody's divorce and then have your kid ask that person about it in a loud voice in a restaurant. I practically break out in a rash when I think about that one. So anyway, thanks to my daughter I was isolated. If I'd identified with even one of those people at the meeting, talking to them might have been a good idea; but I didn't.

Then I thought of an alternative.

+++

I got on Facebook, typed in ADHD, and lists of groups came up. I took my picture off my profile and signed up, just to see what it was like.

OMG there really are people like me with kids like mine. People were questioning each other. "Does anybody else's eight-year-old scream and kick and stop eating for days?" "My four-year-old has bitten a teacher, what should I do?" "I can't cope. My ADHD son's on meds but I can't manage him. I'm depressed for the first time in my life. Am I just a bad parent?"

I dared to ask a question. "My whole life is dictated by my daughter. I cry all the time. Is this normal? Does everybody cry sometimes?"

Five comments later the answers started coming in.

"All the time, kiddo,"replied Evelyn R, leaving a smiley and a thumbs-up.

"It comes in waves. Our son's nearly fourteen. His meltdowns are hell. I fall apart and I'm covered in bruises. My husband has had to give up work and the income support goes nowhere." Annie

"Last year I couldn't get out of bed for a week. My husband did everything. I probably had a breakdown. We plod on because we have to." Janine

"Of course I cry. My ex has walked out and today my son tried to set fire to the shed."

I learned a lot. People were in worse situations than mine. Some had been living with kids who'd been diagnosed with ADHD (and sometimes autism or Aspergers as well) since they were toddlers.

I went to bed late that night. I found myself reviewing Chloë's whole history. Had she really been eight before ADHD set in? She'd been thrown out of schools before that. And at shows – there had been bad behaviour at horse shows. I hadn't remembered these incidents for years but when she was seven, if her pony stalled at an obstacle she'd drop the reins, jump off and flounce out of the ring leaving him standing there. That had happened more than once in front of judges. At the time I'd have described her character as 'tempestuous' or 'strong-willed'. Love is blind. Love conquers reason and so does pride. I hadn't been able to see that she was anything other than normal because she was my daughter, and therefore there could be nothing wrong with her. In my mind, people who had mentally ill children were different from me. I – a competent high achiever – wasn't that sort of person.

That spring the Facebook forum consoled me. They reinforced things I'd already been told, such as the fact that anxiety was what made Chloë so volatile. Desperate to control everything, when she couldn't, she lashed out. I was getting a stream of tips and tactics about how to help her from real people, parents, who'd tried and tested them with problem children of their own. I could be myself and get advice from people who didn't know me or judge me. I found out about medication and what happens when a dose is too high or too low.

So I had Facebook, I had Judy, and I had medication for Chloë. The dose was slowly going up. Dr Salt came to the house, saw my angry daughter in her natural habitat, and raised the medication to 36mg of Concerta after the visit. She also arranged an autism test for early in March.

We were seeing her every couple of weeks. She told me again, as Judy did, that increasing the dose might bring out other symptoms, and she believed that Chloë might be 'on the autism spectrum'. I didn't fully understand what that was. All I knew was that thanks to the pills, I no longer had Chloë-as a-donkey leaping on the furniture croaking Eee-aw, running up and down stairs twenty or thirty times, or blowing bubbles into my face from six inches away. She hadn't hidden in a drawer or thrown her sister about like a paper aeroplane recently. And she was sleeping well.

Meds were a hundred times better than no meds, but the dose wasn't high enough yet. These days she didn't really kick off until she got home. Then she was rude and argumentative, screamed at me if the dogs barked, and talked very loudly at a terrific speed. Also, she was noticeably putting on weight.

'She's too heavy for her pony. He's been bucking –
trying to throw her off his back. But for me the worst
thing is trying to calm her down after school. It's
awful – I just wish I could show you what it's like.
Could we get CCTV?'

'No, 'fraid not. It would be an invasion of privacy.
Don't even go there.'

Dr Salt and Judy agreed that I did need more help
in managing these issues as I would have to live with
them, at least until the dosage plan was perfected.
Social Care (Key Mover: Unsmiling Pauline Race) sent
a Family Worker around who 'may have dealt with
behavioural children'. She was terribly well spoken,
about fifty and perfectly groomed with crimson
shellac nail varnish. No bag-and-briefcase combo for
her. She turned up when Chloë was at school and sat
tense on the edge of the sofa, sipping coffee and
listening. I described the diagnosis and some of
Chloë's 'sensory issues'. She nodded knowingly as I
tried to tell her how it was.

'You see Chloë doesn't think she's got a problem.
She did at one time, but now she thinks she's perfectly
rational. *Anything* can make her kick off. She finds it

difficult at first when she's with people she doesn't know. And she really, really hates noise. You have to keep your voice down. If the TV's on the volume's got to turned off. Taps must never be allowed to drip. And she goes crazy if she hears the dogs' claws tapping on the floor – '

'Don't over-react,' the Family Worker said. 'There is a solution to all this. We run group sessions for children with behavioural problems. She should come along to some of those.'

Really? Had she heard a word I said? 'Chloë hates noise and being with new people' was surely not in code? Did I have to spell out the truth that if Chloë hates something she'll shriek, throw things, be disruptive? And I hadn't even mentioned the latest sensory stuff, like screaming and shouting if a headlamp shone into her eyes when I was driving. Or if I left the bathroom door open while I was brushing my teeth. Or if her food wasn't cut up into mouthfuls and placed on one particular plate with no part of it touching any other. Or if a drink appeared without a straw. A whole range of infuriations was on show when she came home from school.

I was on Facebook that night (still seething after
I'd seen off the Family Worker) and I asked what
drugs other people's thirteen-year-olds were on. It
was always methylphenidate in one form or another:
Ritalin, Concerta, or one of several more. Some were
getting higher doses than Chloë, some less. It didn't
seem age-dependent and since every child exhibited
different behaviours and was physically different, I
couldn't really know whether Chloë's 36mg was high
or low. The aim was to settle the child at a
maintenance dose that would best deal with the
individual's issues, which could vary over time. The
difficulty lay in discovering whether the Ritalin was
repressing, or provoking, a particular set of
symptoms. In this, every child was an experiment. But
one thing I did notice on Facebook was that some of
these kids were getting a top-up dose at four p.m.

Judy came over in the end and saw Chloë in full
Destroy mode after school. I suggested a top-up. She
said, 'Well, the Concerta's supposed to work for
twelve hours. But everybody's different and you're
right, that isn't happening. I'll talk to Dr Salt for you.'

Result! She was put on a total 45mg, 10mg of which was given at four p.m., and it calmed her down. When I got the copy of the prescription request to the GP I was glad to see that the Special Educational Needs Co-ordinator at the school was getting the same data.

+++

March arrived, and it was time for the ADOS assessment at which specialists would decide whether or not my daughter was 'on the autism spectrum'. I was only just getting to grips with ADHD, so I was on shaky ground here. As far as I knew, autism had something to do with blinding calculation skills (I'd seen Dustin Hoffman in *Rain Man*). But whenever 'rigidity' or 'compulsion' were mentioned, so was autism. It didn't make much sense to me. I knew they would want to see Chloë on her own, and she wouldn't like that, so I got my mum to come with us. I didn't want to be by myself with Chloë in meltdown mode in the car or the consulting room either.

The appointment was in the Mental Health wing of the hospital that stood next to Dr Salt's office. As we sat in the waiting room a little boy came in with his father, who was clutching a laptop. He sat down and opened it while the boy ran to the playspace in the corner, picked up two big green wooden building blocks and started banging them together. Chloë smacked her hands over her ears and slid to the floor screaming STOP BANGING! STOP BANGING! My mother took one look at me, put a tissue over her mouth and started to sob. Big help there, then. The father bounded across the room, seized the building blocks, led the boy back and opened the laptop for him just as the door opened. Chloë went quiet.

'Chloë?' asked the nurse. Chloë, to my astonishment, reluctantly left the room with her. Mum and I waited. Mum picked up a copy of *Vogue* that was on the table. I cleared unwanted messages off my phone. The little boy and his father were escorted to their own appointment.

About an hour later Chloë came back.

'What happens now?' I asked the nurse,.

'They'll put their assessment in writing and Dr Salt will talk it through with you at your next appointment.'

We all got into the car and drove off. Mum turned round to Chloë in the back seat.

'What happened when you went in there?'

'Nothing much.'

There had been two men and a woman who seemed 'nice'. Chloë had been asked to pull some things out of a bag and make a story out of them. And she was shown a picture and had to talk about it. One of them had asked her 'If someone didn't know how to brush their teeth what would you say to them?'

'Funny question,' my mother murmured.

'It is,' I agreed. 'What would you have said?'

'I s'pose, squeeze toothpaste onto the brush, and brush up and down, like that, and round and round and make sure you do the backs as well as the fronts. Then do it a couple more times with just water and spit it all out.'

'I didn't say any of that,' Chloë announced. 'I said I'd tell the person If you don't know, don't bother.'

When we got home there was a letter. The IST team, that is, Judy and Simon, would be 'withdrawn as from Monday' because the allotted twelve weeks of intensive support was over. I burst into tears. I had to push, all over again. I tracked down their boss. I begged, I pleaded, I wept. Sorry; rules were rules and the rule was, twelve weeks, and we were no longer 'in crisis' so .... If there was any further need, I'd have to re-apply, or rather the psychiatrist would have to, on our behalf.

+++

Weekends were the worst. Chloë would lie in bed in the morning long past the time when she usually had her pill, but I'd have to go up to the yard so I would wake her up before I left. If that happened she would resolutely pretend to be asleep. If I touched her, or the bedclothes, she kicked and swore and screamed violent abuse in a manic, rough voice, sometimes while smashing furniture or breaking window blinds. I would have to plead with her to take the pill, sometimes for half an hour at a time. Sometimes even bribes didn't work. I started recording these exchanges. She knew I was taping them on my phone but she didn't care.

One Saturday I gave up , went to the yard early, and came back at midday. She still wasn't up but I couldn't face an argument yet. I sat at the kitchen table to write a shopping list. She came in in her dressing gown and started opening cupboard doors, leaving them open.

'Nothing – to – have. With – my – pasta.'

'Well you can't have mini sweet corn.'

'WELLNOBECAUSE**YOU**DECIDEDTOMUNCHIT AWAY THERE IS NODIETFOR YOU YOUPUT SOMEMOREWEIGHT ON SO THEREISNODIETYOU EATALLTHETIME EVERYTHING YOU SEE IN FRONT OF YOU YOU EAT!'

'Just have—'

'NO! You got nothing to eat for my breakfast I'M NOT GOING TO HAVE MY PILL. HONEST. EUGH.'

'What's wrong with cereal?' My voice was dead, defeated. She screamed at me.

'Shuddup don't want CEREAL. Horrible. Same old same old same old thing.'

'Well what's wrong with the pasta?'

'I can't have that alone.'

'Well, put a bit of cheese on it.'

'NO 'cos I DON'T WANT fake plastic cheese. I don't want DAIRY DAIRY DAIRY FAT FAT FAT. Just because YOU eat that doesn't mean I'm gonna want to eat it.'

I pulled myself together.

'Well, I just want you to have your pill.'

'Yeah. Well I just want you to get me some FOOD without you eating it first. Because I can't have a pill without nothink.'

Silence. I wanted to laugh.

I wanted to shoot her.

'Grapes?'

'NO. I don't WANT to bethislittlethingsintime.'

A tangle of nonsense was coming out of her mouth. Silence. She was across the kitchen table, watching me.

'Put sweetcorn on your list.'

'Sweetcorn is on the list.'

'Tiramisu.'

'Tiramisu.'

'Yeah well you bettermakesureyou buy it. Cos – it's on the list; you-have-to-buy-it.'

Rigidity is a presenting characteristic of autism.

'That's not really breakfast, is it?'

'I don't care whatsortofbreakfast ,you're still buying it, cos I've put it on your list. Just like you're gonna buy everythink else that's on your list.'

'Can you just have your pill?'

'NO I CAN'T. I can't have my pill without FOOD.' She was up, slamming cupboard doors. 'You never get nothing in do you?' *Slam.* 'It's your fault.'

I stayed where I was, tears in my eyes.

'I want something to eat.'

'Piece of ham?'

'NO. I don't want a piece of ham. I CAN'T HAVE THAT ON FUCKING PILLS ANYWAY.'

'What about pulled pork?'

'NO. I don't WANT *meat.*'

She banged a cupboard door open and shut, again and again.

'Biscuit?'

'OH SHUT THE FUCK UP AND GO AWAY. NO. Don't want to get those horrible biscuits you buy.'

She wandered off, lay on the sofa, staring at me. Joe was home that weekend, wandered in, picked at the grapes. He looked at her.

'Chlo-ëee....'

'What?'

'You had your pill?'

'No.'

'What about a grape?'

'No.'

'What about a bread roll?'

'No. Don't like bread rolls.'

'What about some Pringles?'

'No, don't like those.'

I say quickly, 'She's got pasta in there that she doesn't want to eat.'

'I don't want pasta on its own. PLAIN OLD FATTY PASTA on its own.'

'You got chicken in there—'

'Mum decided to take all my sweetcorn which she never eats, she doesn't eat this little can of sweetcorn, she eats everything SHE SEES. It's not funny, because it's your fault I ain't had my pill. I'm not having that pasta now, you can have it, cos there's nothing to have it with.'

'Please Chloë just—'

'OH SHADDUP! What d'you think I'll have it with?'

'Just eat it with the pasta—'

'NO! NO! DON'T LIKE PASTA ON ITS OWN.'

Joe said, 'Come with me to the shops quickly and get some sauce, Chloë, and then you can eat your pasta.'

'No. No. '

'Well, just have your pill with a drink.'

'I can't have pills with drinks. They're too big.'

He didn't give up. He opened the fridge.

'What about a yoghurt?'

'No. I don't like yoghurts. Those horrible yoghurts mum gets. I TELL her to get Chocolate Corner Yoghurt but she never does.'

'There's some cheesecake ones and strawberry—'

'Don't like those. I don't like fruit ones or anythink.'

'There's some pineapple chunks,' he said.

'No.'

I was now at the stove. 'Have some sausages.'

Why did I ask? 'OH SHADDUP! MUM! WHYDONTYOULOCKYOURSELF IN?'

'Have a sausage,' said Joe.

'WHAT SAUSAGE?'

'I'm making them, I'm cooking them now,' I told her.

'I don't like them when they've just been cooked.'

'Well I'll blow on them for you.'

'DON'T FUCKING BLOW – NO. NO WAY.

No. No. You're just unhygienic when you cook. That's why I cook my own food. The thought of fucking groggy breath all over my food. EUGH.'

Joe chided her. 'Chloë!' But she'd fixated on me.

'DID YOU WASH YOUR HANDS before you touched those sausages?'

'Please!'

'DID YOU WASH YOUR HANDS?'

'I washed my hands.'

'YOU ARE DISGUSTING.'

'Can you—'

'SHADDUPUPDISGUSTINGEUGH WASHYOURHANDS FORGODSAKE'

'Chloë, hurry up and take your pill.'

'SHADDUP!'

On, and on, it went.

I dreaded weekends. The Saturday morning after the autism test was terrible. She was up, dressed, but she still wouldn't take her pill. I needed to get away from her for ten minutes.

I picked up my car keys.

'I'm going to the shop. I won't be long.'

'I want to come.'

'No. You stay here.'

'NNOOHH!' She hurled her new iPad Air onto the tiled floor and it smashed into pieces.

It had been her birthday present. She loved it. *Oh my God, what'll she be like without that?* She was beginning to frighten me. She ran out of the house.

I picked Gemma up and strapped her into her seat in the car; I called the CAMHS emergency number sobbing. *Please pick up. I need help.* I texted Chloë.

where are you pLEASE COME HOME OR i WILL CALL THE POLICE.

Forty minutes later she came home. I gave her my iPad.

+++

The ADOS assessment had been made. There was to be a big clinical psychology meeting where its outcome would be discussed. I took Chloë to a quick consultation with Dr Salt beforehand, at which we agreed that threatening behaviour towards the baby had stopped, and Chloë seemed slightly more capable of controlling her emotions. I had to reluctantly agree: even the iPod Saturday exchange was mild by comparison with what had gone before. Dr Salt was pleased.

'So,' she said, slipping her papers into a folder, 'let's wind this up and—'

'Hold on,' I said. 'Yes – I've said I've seen improvements. She's better with Gemma, she's sometimes not yelling, but for every time like that, there are three more when she's yelling, or obsessing, or swearing, or refusing – what'd'you call it, 'implacable defiance' – and I can't do anything with her. I—'

'Juliette – I know this is difficult. If—'

'If you don't raise the dose I SHALL SUE. I mean it. I shall sue because the baby and I will be endangered.' I was shaking.

'Calm down, please. Don't – just wait, calm down.'

Dr Salt agreed to increase the dose. There would be 54mg of Concerta (a twelve-hour pill) at eight a.m. and 10mg Ritalin (a four-hour pill) at four p.m., and a couple of melatonin tablets before bed to make sure Chloë got to sleep.

With that decided, the three of us went into a kind of meeting room. There was a low ceiling with a striplight above, a big laminated table. stackable chairs and a whiteboard. I saw a projector in the corner and wished I'd had CCTV to show them.

The other participants were there already: the MHP, the ADHD nurse, the Special Educational Needs woman from Chloë's school, Unsmiling Pauline Race and a man and woman I hadn't seen before. This was where the assessment for autism would be confirmed and a forward plan discussed 'So that we're all on the same page,' Dr Salt said. The man and woman had been among the panel who'd assessed Chloë two weeks ago. They were both clinical psychologists and the woman was a consultant.

Apparently Chloë had seemed anxious that day. She had been uncomfortable with the toothbrushing question and was negative and confused when she was asked to make up a story, complaining that this was the kind of thing she was no good at. But she'd been okay, conversationally. And she didn't flap her hands about.

She'd been unable to identify any emotional experiences of her own and she didn't see them in other people. Asked why people got married, she didn't have a clue. Why they went on holiday, she couldn't imagine. Where money came from, she had no idea. Yes, money got into her bank account. 'I don't know how. It just does.' (I thought maybe she'd simply interpreted that particular question literally, because she certainly knew that I could stop or start the supply – even if she didn't know how I did it, or how the banknotes came to be available.) The verdict was – not creative, not imaginative, unsure about the difference between reality and fiction. She was, because of her gaps in understanding, 'socially vulnerable'.

The Special Ed woman said nothing. Pauline Race took the minutes. As all this was reported, Chloë sat beside me, a small pitiful figure with her coat on and her hood up, trembling.

She definitely had an autistic spectrum disorder. Would knowing that make our lives easier? Well, there was a plan. As backup from now on they'd ask for an ADHD/ASD nurse to be assigned to us. He or she would be prepped by listening to Judy and Simon because they knew us well. Pauline Race would arrange for me to attend a parenting course (there was something called *Raising Teens*). And the consultant clinical psychologist would meet Chloë on her own, to get her to understand that she had two psychological conditions which led her to behave in ways other people could find quite trying.

+++

My daughter's diagnosis was now set out on Chloë's NHS medical record and routinely pasted-in to correspondence.

ADHD

Obsessional behaviour and anxiety, contributing to oppositional behaviour.

Attachment issues

ASD

Sensory issues

Possible learning difficulties

I saw this every time the GP got a letter from Anna or Dr Swan because I was sent a copy. I thought *No one in their right mind will ever consider going out with me and taking this on. I will be single for the rest of my life..... Could it get any worse?*

I didn't bother with *Raising Teens* because it was that uptight Family Worker who rang me up about it and I absolutely did not want, ever again, to sit in a room with a bunch of dead-eyed individuals who'd drifted along in hope of tea and biscuits.

The GP had been asked about an Occupational Therapist, but in our area there was nobody qualified to help with Chloë's sensory issues.

The appeal for transport to school was stuck in the system somewhere.

Judy and Simon came over with the ADHD/ASD nurse. She was going to be available on the phone as Judy had been. I was not impressed, and probably showed it. This woman was older and I was sure she'd never get it. She looked to me like yet another advocate of the well-meaning tea n'biscuits brigade.

On the plus side, when top-up 10mg of Ritalin was prescribed for Chloë after school it stopped the EE-AW noises, the sliding downstairs head first, the sitting under the table and the lie-downs in the chest of drawers. It made her think before grabbing a knife when I said No to her. Her tantrums were fewer, and her intolerance of noise and insistence on certain routines, subsided to vanishing point. We were watching her weight and it was going down. In psychiatry-speak, the top-up was controlling impulsivity, oppositional behaviour, sensory issues and obsessive compulsions. Weird, but exactly as Dr Salt had told me, sometimes higher doses made things worse but higher doses still made them better.

Sigh. After a short lull on the new meds, Chloë's texts began pouring in by the hundred (where was I? who was I with? what was I doing?) and the donkey was back. Until she took her after-school pills she was incredibly volatile. She didn't misbehave at school, but at home I had to tiptoe around her. Anything could set off a tirade of foul-mouthed yelling. We were still seeing Dr Salt every other week, but one night I badly needed to talk to somebody and in despair I gave the ADHD nurse a chance. Turned out she wasn't a dud at all; I'd been unfair to her. She knew her stuff. She was familiar with the medication, the dosage and the effects; also, she told me about parents she'd worked with who'd had to confront the same issues in their children, sometimes for years.

For some reason Chloë resented the ADHD nurse. She'd met her but she wouldn't speak to her and if anything went wrong was that woman's fault.

The psychiatrist and everybody else agreed that Chloë had to accept she had ADHD and ASD. The consultant clinical psychologist, whose name was Anna, was now working on this with her. It was what I really wanted for Chloë, and perhaps myself too. I was on pause; things weren't getting dramatically better but I was managing. However, I was looking to the future all the time and if Chloë stayed in denial, the future looked dismal. At sixteen she'd be legally capable of refusing to take the medication. On the other hand, she really did seem to have bonded with

Anna. I was hopeful that if Anna could lead her to admit she had a problem, she'd recognise her anxiety for the delusion it was. She'd be more willing to relinquish control sometimes, at least.

On the Facebook forum, there were young people as well as parents – girls and boys of eighteen and nineteen who'd spent years on the streets because their parents had thrown them out in exasperation. They told me how they'd got into drugs and got exploited and finally, usually because some charity worker or counsellor had seen their problem for what it was, they'd got treatment. Thinking back, Chloë's call to Childline had been the best thing she ever did. She could have ended on the streets if I hadn't been forced to get help. I'd have thought she was consciously choosing to be abnormally noisy and abusive and impulsive and uncontrollable. I'd never have thought she was mentally ill.

Nobody teaches you the signs of mental illness. Most people wouldn't ever think about it unless it was a plotline in a soap, and anyway they're not going to compare that situation to their own. You love your children so much that you're blind to their faults. It's well known that parents of fat kids don't see them as fat, and it takes a dentist to point out that your child's developing buck teeth and needs a brace.

For years my daughter's primary school were telling me there was 'a problem'. I took no notice. I ignored a long list of really awful things Chloë had done to other children, things she had done to teachers, her rudeness, her behaviour, things she lied about. *She's a child, she'll grow out of it, she's not that bad.*

How do we find out if there's something wrong? We have to tell professionals what our children do, and how they behave. We need a big push to make us do that. The Childline call was my big push.

+++

My life in April 2016 was all about understanding, coping, trying to accept. I was clear about the diagnosis, but I couldn't accept that Chloë might never get better. Both the psychiatrist and the mental health nurse were concerned about me. I was crying all the time. I cried at consultations and I cried on the phone and my daughter told them, irritated, that I was 'always crying'. They booked me with a psychological wellbeing service which would assess my mental state in the course of a half-hour phone call.

Chloë's fourteenth birthday would be in mid-May. She wanted a big party because when Joe's eighteenth came up, he had a party in a night-club, and she remembered that. I wasn't sure what to do because the noise might drive her –literally – crazy.

At the start of May her meds were raised again to 72mg of twelve-hour release Concerta (in two doses daily); one 10mg Ritalin at four p.m. and 4mg of melatonin to help her sleep at bedtime. For several weeks we had no knives, no nastiness, no shouting, no meltdowns, no swinging Gemma about, no bombarding me with text messages, no throwing things at me, no abuse, no walking out of the house, no kicking the dogs, no donkey! I could actually reach a compromise with her. Defying professional advice I let her have the party in the night-club and she coped very well; loved the organising of it and inviting people. She'd wanted it, so she couldn't blame me when she had to suppress her feelings during the event itself. But only those who knew her really well could see the terror in her eyes when she had to stand in the middle of sixty people and listen to them singing *Happy Birthday Dear Chloë*.

It was all going so well. It's true that at this time, at home, she would occasionally sit under the dining table and say something rude at random when people visited (for instance 'I need a big fat juicy turd') or shout 'Why's that man got skinny legs?' But hey, nobody's perfect. Maybe, I thought, she could wear a tee-shirt saying "I'M AUTISTIC" on the front with "*and* ADD" on the back?

Maybe *I* could wear a teeshirt –

Sorry

←→

she's autistic

with ADHD.

Embarrassment was nothing. It was a lot better than the abuse of the past, and even funny, in retrospect. I asked Dr Salt, 'Is she better now? Can I take her off the medication now?'

She just looked at me and quietly said, 'I'm afraid it's the medication that's doing it.'

A life sentence, then. Chloë would always have to take these drugs and I would always have to make sure she did.

'Have you noticed any other changes, from the new dose?'

'Yes,' I admitted. 'The sensory issues have been really bad since the party. The dogs aren't supposed to drink water loudly or walk about on the wood floor or bark. I can't sing along with music in the car, or beat time on the steering wheel. I can't eat anything crunchy while Chloë's next to me because she can't stand the noise. I've taken the clock down from the wall in the hall because of the tick-tock...'

'All symptomatic of autism, then.'

'Yes, and she's got this obsession now, counting calories. She wants to know how many calories are in everything.'

'Has she lost more weight?'

'Yes. She's 53 kilos. She can ride again.'

'That's okay, but the rate of decrease concerns me. It may be too quick. I'll ask your GP to arrange a blood test. And as a precaution I'll take the Concerta back down to 54mg.'

Within thirty-six hours the donkey noises were back and Chloë was terrified, really paranoid –if she ate off a regular plate, her food tasted funny; if she ate using metal cutlery, it clattered in her mouth. She couldn't sleep in her bed, because it was too big. She wanted a single bed. I rang the ADHD nurse who put all this down to Chloë's anxiety. Which was fine as a diagnosis, but all I knew was, I had to get an immediate appointment to get her prescribed 72 mg again.

I got it quickly because Dr Salt had the blood test results. They showed that the meds were not causing weight loss. We talked on the phone. I told her what was going on. She said, 'Well, these things are symptomatic of autism. The obsessive attitude to calories, for instance, and rigid habits about eating and sleeping.'

'She goes up to her room and she can't be disturbed after five o'clock. It's a rule.'

'I see. And how are you managing, Juliette? D'you think you'll be okay when the dose is back to normal? I know you didn't want to do the parenting course.'

'No. I feel much better.' *Might as well keep her happy. What else am I supposed to say?*

+++

How long it would last I didn't know. It would, as usual, be largely up to Chloë. Since babyhood, she'd been instrumental in maintaining or destroying my relationships. I accept that. In my view, children should like their parents' partners. Unfortunately Chloë had never yet liked mine.

In May and June her weight dropped to 49 kilos and she looked fine. She was as stable as she was likely to get on the 72mg dose, plus the after-school Ritalin and the melatonin pre-sleep. I felt happier. I stopped engaging with the Facebook group because I'd begun to see a pattern; lot of people in the forum were endlessly negative. There was a sort of race to the bottom ("my life's worse than yours"). I was no longer in that place.

+++

In the summer term of 2016 things went less well. A Team Around the Child group got involved and for some reason I was assigned an Early Years Helper who obviously hadn't a clue about autism or ADHD – at least, not in a fourteen-year-old; why would she? Why would the bureaucrats who apparently chose her on behalf of the Council think I'd waste my time taking advice from someone who was out of her depth? Maybe it made the Council look as if they were doing something.

Next bloody thing. Dr Salt would be moving on. We were to have a different psychiatrist. I was dismayed beyond words. Chloë could get so unnerved by change. I'd trusted Dr Salt and it had taken months to build a really good relationship on both sides. But I couldn't prevent this change from happening.

In the end Dr Florey, the second psychiatrist, turned out to be fine. We met her in the consulting rooms previously occupied by Dr Salt. She was an older, smiley woman with pepper-and-salt hair in a wispy bun. I thought she'd probably been a hippie, way back.

Chloë was definitely starting to get a bit more stable. Her weight had settled at around 50 kilos. She wanted to be six stone, she told Dr Florey, because it would be better for her pony. She still counted calories obsessively. However, she wasn't eating only six hundred calories a day as she claimed. Dr Florey, faced with the stable weight and Chloë swearing to only six hundred calories, made a note on the computer but looked incredulous. I wasn't about to explain with Chloë there, but the fact was, if my daughter asked me how many calories were in a Big Mac, for instance, I'd say...'Oh, maybe a hundred.'

I think the doctor noticed that I looked as sceptical as she felt, so she moved on.

'So ...has anything else changed?' she asked.

Chloë said, 'There's girls at school. They're nasty to me.'

'How, Chloë?'

'They say things on Facebook and they run away when I see them.'

'How does that make you feel?'

'They're just stupid.'

'What d'you think, Juliette?'

'Chloë can offend people but she has no idea how badly she's hurting them. That's what the ADHD nurse told me, anyway. She said lack of empathy's an autistic symptom.'

'I'm not autistic,' Chloe muttered, kicking the floor with her heels. When she had stopped Dr Florey looked back at me.

'D'you agree about the lack of empathy?'

Well, she'd asked. 'Certainly I do. I'm called thick, fat, horrible on an hourly basis. My hair doesn't look nice, my clothes are the wrong colour. When Chloë's talking to someone else and I'm in the story, she always says something hurtful. I don't think she can know how hurtful it is, or she wouldn't do it.'

'D'you argue with people at school about things like that, Chloë?'

'No.'

Dr Florey waited.

Chloë talked at the floor. 'I know I've got ADHD, and Anna explained all that. But it's okay to be different. I don't see why I'm supposed to have autism as well.'

I said to Dr Florey, 'The thing is, the medication works, but when one set of symptoms go away, another set appears, and usually it's the Insult set.'

'Hm. So what d'you do, Chloë, when your friends run away?'

'I don't care. I don't want to talk to them anyway. They're always shrieking and squealing. I've got my own friends.'

It was true. She did hang out with just one or two friends. She hated big crowds of kids, and she hated noise, which is why she never went to lunch in the school cafeteria but preferred to stay in the classroom. At the same time she wanted to know all the gossip so as not to be left out, and she'd spend hours on Facebook or Snapchat, tracking the lives of girls in her class.

+++

I worked on my reactions to my daughter and by midsummer of 2016, I had a whole new set. I never talked to her while I was driving. I made sure that when she came home from school she'd have the food she wanted right away. I didn't tell her to do things or remind her of time limits any more. These days I said, 'When you're ready.'

I never told her to clear up her room. But then I wanted to do that myself anyway. It gave me more insight into what was happening in her life, and her mind. For instance, I found fake cigarettes. I made no comment. Mostly she hoarded rubbish, squirreled away behind other things. You see TV programmes about hoarders but they're usually eccentric old folk. I was living with one who was fourteen. She stashed all sorts of rubbish – empty boxes, half-finished drinks, dirty underwear, cut hair – yes, cut hair; biros with no ink, years-old toothbrushes, worn-out toys. Keeping things as a barrier, maybe, or keeping things so that everything stayed the same? I didn't know. Anxiety, though.

At one time, I'd have gone into a panic about how all this junk would attract mice, or cockroaches. I'd now stopped expressing outrage. Above all I had to let Chloë feel in control. So I just accepted rubbish-hoarding as a fact of life and quietly disposed of anything that might go mouldy or smell.

I decided to sell her pony. Chloë was losing interest, and didn't seem to mind; and the animal's welfare had to be my main concern. We were in a tranquil phase at the moment but I no longer dared to expect it to last.

Dr Florey and the ADHD nurse were worried because I still wept at appointments. I couldn't stop grieving for the affectionate little girl I'd once had. Sometimes at the weekend I delayed the pill for an hour and she wasn't angry when I cuddled her or gave her a kiss. For that hour I could pretend I'd got her back. And then I'd see subtle changes, and I'd know she'd have to have her pill or she'd kick off.

Dr Florey was good but didn't stay long – after only two appointments she was already off to a new post. I was informed by letter that Chloë would become a patient of Dr Ray Uxter in August.

Her third psychiatrist in eight months... I needed to offload a lot of annoyance and frustration. I rang the ADHD nurse, who usually managed to talk me down.

'Who makes these decisions?' I wanted to know.

'I don't know, to be honest. Somebody in CAMHS.'

'Don't we have any rights in this?'

'Not until she's sixteen. Under the Mental Capacity Act, a person who can make a decision for themselves is supposed to be able to decide what kind of treatment they get, and their carers get listened to as well. But it only applies to over-sixteens. So you and Chloë are stuck with CAMHS for now.'

'So somebody who doesn't know her has made this decision for an autistic ADHD child who doesn't like change when she's only just learned to trust a new person.'

'That's how it works, I'm afraid.'

'But if all these kids are different, how are psychiatrists ever going to understand them and help them if they don't stay long enough to get to know them? They surely can't think that they've done their job once the child has a label, and from then on they can give them the standard treatment for that label?'

'Well, if they work in mental health they're supposed to know about the need for continuity. I guess sometimes circumstances make that difficult.'

'And is this a man or a woman? Ray Uxter. It could be either.'

'It's a man. I've never met him, he's new.'

'Oh my God. She gets on better with women.'

'Well... I completely understand where you're coming from. But unless you want to make a formal complaint I don't think there's anything you can do. He'll have read the file and I just hope Chloë can develop a rapport with him.'

+++

Off I drove again. Chloë was used to this particular hour-long journey now, having made it, by my calculation, about sixteen times. My iPad kept her occupied in the back seat.

As usual, the appointment was at three p.m. on a Monday. The security man at the desk was an old acquaintance. I signed myself in and he took us to the consulting room. A pudgy be-suited man in his

thirties, Dr Uxter got up, beaming, to shake hands
with us.

'Hi, I'm Ray. Hi Juliette! Hi Chloë! Make yourselves
comfortable.... ' We all sat down. Unlike the other
psychiatrists he didn't sit behind the desk, but invited
us to sit with him around the coffee table. 'Well,
you've been having quite a time of it, haven't you? I've
been reading the file.' He made it sound quite
thrilling. He wore his hair gelled up on top and shaven
at the sides. Cheesy, I thought. Did he think it made
him look younger? If so he was mistaken. He was still
talking.

'How d'you feel about the care Chloë's receiving,
Juliette?'

'Well, I'd have liked to maintain continuity. It's
hard enough to learn to trust a psychiatrist without
having the face in front of you change every few
months. And Chloë's done very well so far but she
can't keep developing relationships if they're gonna
just ...disappear.'

He nodded earnestly. 'I completely get that. I'm
sorry but it's a time of radical change in the mental
health service and I saw from your reports how hard

things have been. But we are where we are, and from now on, you'll see me.' Unlike Dr Salt and Dr Florey, he wasn't taking notes. Behind him his desk was cluttered with folders and papers, a phone on charge and an in-tray, but the computer was off. He was riffling through Chloë's file.

'Chloë's lost weight rather quickly, yeah?'

'Yes, but she had put on a lot. Now she's pretty much back to normal.'

'Well yeah but you see – ' He leaned back in his chair, fingertips together over his small paunch. I settled in for the long haul. 'I have to tell you, I suppose I want to reassure you, but I am a biologist as well as a psychiatrist. In fact my first degree was in biology, before I did a master's in neurobiology at Imperial, and qualified after that in psychiatry. So, biology is so to speak my first love. And it gives me particular insights into the physical workings of some of the medications we use. Now looking through your file I spotted the difficulties you've been having in getting the correct dosage for Chloë. You may have noticed that sometimes when methylphenidate is *over* prescribed, it works antagonistically. That's to say, the result is the opposite of what the doctor intended.'

'I know that,' I said, fed up with his conceit – he'd barely looked at Chloë, never mind talked to her – 'but Dr Salt and Dr Florey have spent eight months getting the dose right and they pretty much have. The 72 mill of Concerta plus the 10 mill of Ritalin keeps things under control, more or less.'

'I'm afraid I don't see it. The anxiety is still there, isn't it?'

'No. ...Well – Yes, of course it is, but she's vastly better than she was a year ago. Before Christmas last year she was almost – ' I wanted to say 'suicidal' but I couldn't with Chloë beside me. 'Are you saying you think she's being over-prescribed? Because I can tell you she isn't. She's getting the right treatment.'

'It can get better. It may seem counter-intuitive to you but trust me, I have expertise in this field. She is on the maximum for her age. If the dose is reduced, we can fine-tune –'

I couldn't believe I was hearing this.

'Please. Stop. I *can't* take her off the medication. I can't cope with her off the medication.' I felt tears spring to my eyes and my voice was rising. 'Dr Salt spent six months seeing my daughter every other week. She even came to the house. An Intensive Support Team were coming round twice a week. And when Chloë went off the medication, because she refused to take it, Social Services very nearly removed her from the family because of the danger to her baby sister. And now you want to change everything? Move backwards? Wasn't Dr Florey just as well qualified as you? You've read the file, well you say you've read the file, don't you *believe* how bad she was? Because the IST came and confirmed it. I'M NOT TAKING HER OFF THE MEDICATION! I WON'T LET YOU REDUCE THE DOSE!'

'Juliette, Juliette,' he said. He reached for a box of tissues from the desk behind him and passed it across to me. 'Of course I believe the file. It's all on the record. But I want you to think about Chloë's situation.' *Like I'd been doing anything else for the past eighteen months.* 'Can you confirm that Chloë has *never* stopped being anxious? Can you?'

'Yes.'

'Then I want you to think about why that might be. Because it doesn't have to be the *level* of the dose. It could be the *type* of dose. Maybe methylphenidate is the wrong drug at the moment.'

I dabbed at my eyes and composed myself. 'There's no alternative.'

'That's not necessarily a constructive view. Ideally the alternative is to find out why the anxiety is present and treat that. It seems to underlie everything. The need for control, the oppositional behaviour, the rigid habits, everything is at bottom rooted in anxiety and fear. What I need, if we're going to help Chloë, is your commitment to work with me. To go forward and find out the cause.'

'And then what?'

'Well, we treat it. There are many alternatives. It could be a talking cure, or a different drug or a lesser prescription or – if a talking cure worked, then it could be no prescription at all. There are people with a similar diagnosis in childhood who have grown into fully functioning adults.'

He went on in this vein. I didn't have anything much to say; I was confused. He agreed to let me think about it. 'We'll give it time. See you again in two weeks.'

So we left. I did think about it. I was undecided. When I saw things his way, I felt I'd crossed high mountain after high mountain, dark valley after dark valley, and now I'd reached the horizon and a wonderful sunlit view lay before me.

But could I reduce the dose and risk going through hell again? No.

On the other hand, maybe if we did just understand Chloë better, and shift her mind-set to recognising what was wrong, her label would fall away. And then she would be happy like other children. If so, maybe the experiment would be worth it?

But then Anna had been working with Chloë for months now and getting Chloë's self-image to change was a very slow business. Surely it wouldn't help to mess that up by changing the medication?

I didn't know what to think. He cancelled the second appointment. When we finally saw him at the start of September, he seemed a bit vague and pre-occupied, I thought. We discussed Chloë's underlying anxiety but he'd stopped going on about the medication.

+++

These days, when Chloë saw Anna alone for half an hour I spent the time with the ADHD nurse; and then we swapped over. It worked well, because if either of them saw us together, Chloë would start an argument with me and we'd get nothing done.

In September Chloë started getting homework from Anna. She had to write up the discussions they were having about things she was best at and things she liked, and things she found difficult or disliked. This was part of helping her accept her autism-spectrum-disorder and attention-deficit-hyperactivity-disorder. At another meeting she had to present an essay on the research she'd been asked to do into ASD and ADHD. She was rightly proud of this and read it aloud to me. Unfortunately it made me cry. Perhaps I was the one who should be on medication?

One afternoon when Chloë was with the ADHD nurse, Anna asked me how she was getting on at school.

I hadn't given it much thought. In view of what had gone before, no news was good news. 'To be honest I don't really know,' I said. 'With CAMHS appointments every week, looking after the horses and the clients, looking after Gemma, trying to keep Chloë on track, cooking for all of us – Joe was doing work experience about fifteen miles from us until last week, he's only just gone back to London yesterday and I was ferrying him there and back as well as getting Chloë to school– the transport department people at the council won't give her a bus ticket, so I've had to appeal again – you see there's a lot going on. Honestly, I haven't been paying attention.'

'It does sound a bit demanding. But I have to tell you what she told me. Now she's in the fourth year, maths is really hard for her.'

'She was always good at maths.'

'Yes, but as autistic children advance in certain subjects they do find them difficult. It's because autism usually implies an inability to handle metaphor. For instance, if I asked an autistic child to go and jump in the bath she'd climb into the bath fully clothed and jump up and down. And when you get to a certain level, maths becomes more abstract. It's not that they can't learn, but they learn differently. Teachers need special training to explain some concepts to autistic children. It can be done. Autistic children can be outstanding at maths but they need specialised tuition.'

'Well, maybe I should ask the school?'

'There's probably a Special Educational Needs Co-ordinator at Chloë's school? SENCO, they're called.'

'Yes. Well, I know there is one. I met her once. But she's hopeless. She had no idea what I was talking about.'

'Ask her if there's a Working Together Team near you. They're teachers trained in communicating effectively with kids like Chloë. They go into mainstream schools and teach other teachers how to do it. This woman will talk to them if you push her gently in their direction.'

That night I found the County's education page on its website. There was a Working Together Team. It offered a free service and, unbelievably, it operated out of the school that was right next door to the one Chloë went to.

The next day I rang them up and explained the situation. The man who answered confirmed everything Anna had said. Yes, they trained teachers to teach children like Chloë.

'So have you worked with anybody at her school?'

'No, we haven't.'

' Why's that? I mean, seventeen hundred kids go to it. Chloë can't be the only autistic one.'

'True. But we haven't been asked. We need a referral.'

'Who makes the referral?'

'Usually the SENCO, and the parent has to sign it off.'

'Okay, so the SENCO's there and I've got her email. If I ask her to refer Chloë, will you train a teacher to help her?'

'Absolutely. I've got the referral forms here so you can pick one up. Actually we're having a monthly meeting for parents with autistic children tomorrow. You can come along and meet us if you like. Ask for me, I'm Tom.'

I went along at ten a.m., collected my referral paperwork and met Tom. He wasn't a mental health professional – somehow I'd thought he would be. But he was a teacher, and he'd taken some courses in teaching autistic kids, so he was better qualified to teach Chloë than others on the staff. Well, I thought, it's a start.

He took me into a room and I was briefly introduced to a smattering of other parents and four teachers. Alongside us were the usual tea-urn and enough biscuits on paper plates to open several retirement homes. We sat facing a flatscreen TV.

Tom was watching me fixedly as a five-minute video began. Four different children explained their autistic issues. Some of them experienced life exactly the way my daughter did. I was welling up again. I covered my eyes and tried to pull myself together. I felt disconnected. I didn't want this to be real. The five minutes seemed to go on and on. I didn't want to accept that these kids, these poor kids, were just like my poor Chloë.

When it ended Tom briskly told us what he did and how he would be teaching other teachers to do the same in the schools where our children learned. Once I'd listened to him I was absolutely satisfied that he knew what he was talking about. At the end, I fled as usual before people started mingling and drinking tea. I wanted all the privacy I could find.

Mrs Smith the SENCO teacher eventually emailed and gave me a date when we could meet, two weeks away. Then in a second email she informed me that our appointment would have to be put back a further week, as Mrs Marshall, the Deputy Head of the next-door school – the one where Working Together was based – had asked to come along. She was a SENCO too and in the new year, the two schools would be merging.

Eventually, I had a meeting with both of them. I had a big pink folder on my lap, full of correspondence and reports on Chloë. I don't know what it was about that particular day but I was on a roll: absolutely fired up with resentment towards the barely-there SENCO from Chloë's school.

'What exactly do you do here? Because far as I know you haven't helped my daughter.'

'Well I am qualified to work with special needs children up to GCSE level, and I do. But Chloë has so far managed to keep up with the mainstream class, so she's not really a special needs pupil.'

The Deputy Head pre-empted my angry response. She quickly said, 'I'm an S.E.N. Co-ordinator too. Mrs Smith and I will be working together during the transition, so is there any way I can help?'

'I hope so. My daughter is clever, but because she's on the autism spectrum she has trouble understanding maths. Over at your school there's a Working Together team. They teach teachers to teach kids with mental health issues from mainstream schools. That's what they do. There is no cost. They're two hundred yards away. I can't understand why Mrs Smith has never approached them.'

Mrs Marshall looked at her. I looked at her.

'Well as I said—'

'What are you actually paid to do?'

'Well—'

'Because my daughter needs specialist help, and you've ignored her. In this folder there are letters and reports from a GP, three psychiatrists, two clinical psychologists, about ten other mental health professionals of one kind or another, and about as many teachers. Chloë sees a psychiatrist every other week, she sees a clinical psychologist every other week and she's on the maximum dose of methylphenidate for her age. 72 milligrams of Concerta every day, 10 mill of Ritalin to deal with her freakouts after school, melatonin to get her to sleep. Do you actually understand what this means? What a worry it is for me and how careful your attitudes have to be around a child like this?'

She sat stunned. She said nothing.

'I think I've seen some of those CAMHS letters, Janet. They're on your desk downstairs. Would you mind making a couple of copies of each of them for me?'

The SENCO scuttled out, her face pink. I didn't care. She'd been dismissive of Chloë's problems, so why should I? Mrs Marshall apologised and suggested that I should put a complaint in writing.

'Chloë's getting on well in other subjects, is she?'

'Most of them, yes. She's a clever girl. But the autism makes her literal-minded, so she needs special tuition with maths – do you know Tom at the Working Together team?'

'Yes, of course.'

'Well, he'll explain but – maths is important, but she's been completely lost this term, and she's started copying her friend's work. Also she's got a permanent underlying anxiety that makes her panicky and confrontational if she's told to work against the clock. She gets really agitated. And she hates being in a crowd so if she has to do a GCSE exam in a huge exam room to a deadline with a hundred other kids round her – '

The SENCO woman came back into the room flapping a piece of paper. She blurted

'I did a SENDS report in February this year and her point scoring was fine.'

'In February,' I said through gritted teeth, 'Chloë was on less than half the dose of ritalin she's getting now. She hadn't even been diagnosed with autistic spectrum disorder then. She has acute sensory issues around noise and they've got worse. Why would you think one report is enough? Mental health changes over time. Some of Chloë's school reports say she answers questions very quickly, as if she's guessing. Why would you *not* think that indicates something wrong?'

I don't think the SENCO had a great day. But I'd pushed hard, and at least I knew she'd have to do something to help at last. In a way, I felt doubly triumphant about that. I could never have been so assertive before Chloë's medication really started to do some good. When Chloë was at her worst, on no dose or a lower dose, I'd felt too overwhelmed by misery to express my anger properly.

+++

I was quite looking forward to the fourth appointment with Dr Uxter. Chloë didn't like him and I was still suspicious, but he had not insisted on reducing the medication, she was still stable, and he did seem very enthusiastic about wanting to find out what made her so anxious. He'd even asked her a few questions at last. So if he could find out what her fears really were while the medication was helping her focus, that would be fine with me.

He began the session by handing me a leaflet on drugs used to treat ADHD. Then he leaned back and said, 'I have been thinking about the side effects of Concerta, the obsessional behaviour around food and so on.'

'The calorie counting.'

'Yes, that and other things. Maybe even the dysphoria.'

'The what?'

'The underlying anxiety. There's a drug called fluoxetine. It's an SSRI, which means it increases the levels of a neurotransmitter called serotonin in the brain. Serotonin among other things reduces anxiety levels.'

'But Chloë's current prescription is working.'

'Up to a point. We've talked about side effects. The pills Chloë is taking are for ADHD specifically. They're all ritalin in some form and they work differently, via the central nervous system.'

'I don't see that makes much difference, as long as they reduce the impulsivity and the aggression and help her focus.'

'That does seem to be true, but she is on the highest possible dose. I'm sure you can see the benefits but the side-effects will take their toll.'

He was probably right. And I could see that the 'benefits' were skin-deep; if I didn't absolutely tiptoe around Chloë her aggression reappeared.

'So you think she should be taking fluoxetine.'

'I do, and that's what I shall be prescribing, with your agreement.'

'To make her less anxious.'

'Yes.'

'Okay then. I can see that if she's less anxious she won't have these issues.'

'Good. The two benefits together should achieve that. I'll have to reduce the Concerta beforehand—'

'Oh no! No, I can't have the Concerta reduced. Not at all.'

'Believe me, Juliette, I am trying to help Chloë. But you know what the issue is. She will need to manage her own mental health as she gets older. We have to address the underlying anxiety with fluoxetine in order to get her to that point. I know you want nothing more than for her to be in a better place, mentally.'

'And you have to reduce the Concerta so that you can switch her to fluoxetine next time?'

'Exactly.'

'If she ever misses even one dose she's very aggressive again – it did happen—'

'There is nothing, believe me, nothing to worry about. She will still be on 45 milligrams a day.'

My jaw dropped. Back to my nightmare life – no.

'45 milligrams is 27 milligrams less than she's getting! Why not just one step back to 54?'

'I'm afraid that's how we have to do it. I can't leave her on a dose as high as 54 milligrams before she switches to fluoxetine. Don't worry. She'll be a lot less volatile, and if anything's wrong just call me. I'll make myself available at any time. And I want you to keep a daily log, if you wouldn't mind. Just for this initial two weeks.'

Did I push back? No. I agreed.

+++

I did keep a log, though looking back, I wondered why I bothered – the other psychiatrists had put everything in writing to me and our GP within days of our appointments, but Uxter – who didn't keep notes, so he had none to write up – had only ever sent one such letter. He just wanted me to do the work.

LOG. (Extracts.)

Day 2. Friday.

All hell has broken loose. She's complaining about her eyes. She can't open them in the morning. They're streaming with water. 'You must have hayfever,' I say. SHUDDUP SHUDDUP I BLOODY DON'T. And so on in a tantrum for forty minutes. YOU DON'T CARE ABOUT ME, YOU DON'T LOOK AFTER ME, YOU'RE SUPPOSED TO BE MY FUCKING MOTHER AND YOU DON'T – and so on. I leave her to it and go downstairs. I call the optician. I go back into her room where she's under the bedclothes. Stick my head around the door.

'Okay, you've got an appointment at Specsavers at four thirty on Tuesday.'

'THAT'S NO FUCKING USE. I need it now.'

'No chance.'

'I need it TOMORROW and what the fuck use is four thirty when I have stuff to do then? I want it tomorrow morning.'

I call another optician and get her the appointment she wants.

This evening the donkey arrived. No EE-AW. Just hand and leg movements. I smiled.

She smiled back as if to say, 'Can't be helped; have to do it.'

Day 3. Saturday

To the optician. He too suggests hayfever. Chloë's not having it. He prescribes some gel she has to put on in the mornings.

This eye thing is something she didn't get when she was on 45mg before. Maybe a side effect?

She spends most of the day in her room.

This evening she's bouncing off walls, wanting to play-fight with me, poking me to get a reaction.

Day 4. Sunday.

She hasn't eaten since yesterday morning. Screaming at me from her room.

Day 6. Tuesday.

Two foul days. Chloë had a meeting with Anna yesterday but she wouldn't sit on the

chair, just on the floor, so Anna isn't making
another appointment until we get a
prescription that works. I haven't kept a log.
Chloë looks terrible; skinny and exhausted.
After school today – I'm in the garden, trying
to keep clear. She's shouting about some
clothes that she can't find. She's screaming.
She hates me. She wants to live somewhere
else. She kicks the dogs as she goes past them.

I can't take this any more. I'm crying. I
want her back on the normal dose. From the
garden, I call the psychiatrist. He's *not bloody
there*. And his phone's switched off. They offer
me an emergency appointment to see another
psychiatrist.

'NO. I need Dr Uxter to put my daughter
back on the meds she was on before. He knew
this might happen. He promised to be
available if I called.' I end the call, furious.
Chloë comes outside shouting abuse.

'I'm not taking ANY MORE FUCKING
PILLS JUST BECAUSE YOU WANT ME TO!'

'Go indoors. Leave me alone.'

'NO. I want to know what you're saying on the phone.'

I put my phone in my pocket. She goes back, walks to the front door and slams out of the house.

I call CAMHS again demanding to speak to someone who can help me. I go through the whole thing again, about how my psychiatrist promised I would be able to contact him in an emergency, but I am now at crisis point, and he's not there, and now the patient has gone AWOL.

'Have you reported her missing?'

'No. She's not missing. She'll just walk round the village. She'll be back soon enough. But without the proper meds she's in no condition to look after herself. And she's verbally abusive.'

They put me through to a duty psychiatrist called Paul with an extraordinarily calming voice. I hang on while he reads Chloë's notes to himself. After four or five minutes –

'Thank you for waiting,' he says. 'I want to know – why did Dr Uxter reduce the dose of Concerta?'

'He wanted to put her on fluoxetine so he had to reduce it. What she needs now is her daily Concerta put back to 72 milligrams. I don't care if she never takes the fluoxetine as long as she gets the Concerta.'

'Then by all means put her back on the 72 milligrams right away. Only stop if you notice adverse effects. It won't affect any future dose of fluoxetine. The two things work in completely different ways. Some patients take both at once.'

I gasped. 'Then why on earth did Dr Uxter tell me I had to reduce it?'

'I have no idea,' Paul says.

He's faxing a further prescription to Boots so I can pick it up in the morning. Chloë will have enough to see her through to the appointment next week. Intend to ask Uxter what the hell he thought he was doing. Trauma of past week has been totally unnecessary. I'm giving up this log. It's Uxter's job to keep records, not mine.

+++

I didn't have time to sit and seethe. Chloë still hadn't come home. I texted her 'Come back. I have an offer to make.' She came back. She'd been walking for about an hour and was much calmer.

From tomorrow morning I'd raise the dose to its former level. I did what she'd understand: I gave her a written contract.

I Juliette Mare agree that Chloë Mare will receive £20 per week in her bank if:

She takes 2 x 27mg and 1 x 18mg concerta (12 hour release)

1 x 10mg of Ritalin at 4pm (4 hour release)

With no arguments.

If these terms are breached without medical advice, payments will stop.

Signed & dated _____

Juliette Mare

I agree to the above terms.

Signed & dated _____

Chloë Mare

This I think amused her and although there were a few bounces and giggles she signed it.

The ADHD nurse rang the next day wanting to confirm the return to 72mg, and I explained. Also I told her what I thought of Dr Uxter, leaving a parent on her own to supervise her lunatic child's reaction to a drastic chemical change. Especially as he knew I was a busy woman with a baby. I was still so cross that I wrote to the Director of Children's Clinical Services and complained. The Director didn't reply, but I did find out that he'd sent copies to the ADHD nurse and the psychiatrist.

So our next appointment with Uxter was uncomfortable. The ADHD nurse sat in on it. I no longer trusted this man. I demanded to know why he'd reduced the dose to 45mg when everything in Chloë's file, and everything I'd told him, indicated that this would be a bad idea.

'I'm her psychiatrist now so I needed to see for myself' he said. I don't like complacency.

'You mean you wanted *me* to re-run an experiment that already failed, as you should have known from the files. I was supposed to do this in *my* time, with my vulnerable baby and my vulnerable animals in the house. If you really wanted to see for yourself you could have visited us to see the effects. Dr Salt did. That's how she found out Chloë needs a high dose.'

He sighed. 'Shall we not revisit all that? I would like to move on, if you don't mind. Chloë's school has supplied me with her Connors behaviour score. It shows that she's doing well, so I won't be changing any medication at this time.'

'May I see it?'

He turned his papers around. There was a graph and a lot of tick-boxes.

I told him. 'I've seen these before. Two of the earlier ones were not filled in properly. This looks the same to me. They get filled in by teaching assistants. Or somebody else. But not by the people who actually teach Chloë. That's why they make no sense. They make it look as if she's an angel at school but I don't believe it. The same girl can't be an angel at school and a devil at home. The pills help her concentrate but they don't change her underlying issues. The underlying behavioural issues can't show up unless the form is filled in by people who teach her and know her.'

'These are the scores I have to work with, Juliette. I have to take notice of the school's professional opinion.'

'The S.E.N Co-ordinator there is incompetent!' I protested. He surreptitiously looked at his watch. 'And the clinical psychologist agrees that Chloë's getting frustrated by maths, for instance, because she's not taught by specialists who understand her disability—'

'Juliette,' he interrupted, raising his voice. 'We have to wrap this up now.'

I stood up and shouted, 'Your reports are a load of old tosh. It's not a true reading.'

He asked the ADHD nurse to take Chloë out of the room and wait outside. When we were alone he said

'Do you want Chloë to be treated by a different psychiatrist?'

'You're not listening. I don't think you're capable of listening.'

I left.

+++

The following day two letters arrived from the school. They'd been posted on different dates. They confirmed that my daughter had been detained in isolation twice. This was because she'd been given detention for disruptive behaviour, interrupting the teachers and disturbing the class, but she hadn't stayed to do the detention on either occasion.

I called CAMHS and asked for Chloë to be assigned a different psychiatrist. I couldn't blame

Uxter alone for Chloë's antisocial reaction when he
messed up the prescription, but he should have been
able to read between the lines of the notes. Maybe he
had too little time, or he just wasn't a subtle enough
person to see that without the right meds, this girl
was way beyond any parent's capacity to handle.
Especially one with a toddler and horses to look after.

And yet – probably the most scary thing about all
this was that when she was good, she was funny.
Really funny, self-deprecating. She'd send me pictures
and knowingly winning little messages

puzzle on offer from £90 to £40.

i'll do all your poo picking <u>tomorrow</u>.

for u to buy it for me <u>tomorrow</u>.

as <u>offer ends very soon</u>

i'll do all ur poo picking first

all the fields <u>tomorrow</u>

and i'll hack ur horse <u>tomorrow</u>

and i'll ride Lola and Jenny and Wisty <u>tomorrow</u>

and u buy me that puzzle <u>tomorrow night</u>

please

that puzzle keep me entertained and quiet for the rest of my life

i'll do it in my own bedroom

i'll be good

i'll take my pill without u having to ask me...

+++

I thought the system was really to blame. The psychiatrist who had diagnosed Chloë, who got to know me as a mother and a person, who saw how we lived, should have been allowed to continue her care. It's impossible for mental health professionals to understand the individual child and parent if they don't spend enough time with them. I understand that time is something psychiatrists don't have; but these children often behave in ways that aren't in any textbook. The parents on Facebook, and any other parents I've met, instinctively feel that if you understand *why*, you can start to understand how to divert or modify behaviour. They ask the sort of things I've asked. Why their child texts forty-five times in one day asking about stir-fry and chips. Why they hiss like a cat if they don't want to hear what their mum is telling them. Why they hate being interrupted. Why they dislike the mouth-feel of cutlery. Why they talk too fast to be understood. Why they're happy to live in a tip but must always look immaculate.

Why when they want something they can be funny and charming.

Why they are hateful to their parents but cling to them as well.

+++

Just before Christmas my constant badgering of the County Council's transport committee – the one that had turned down my application for school transport at least four times – agreed to meet me face to face. I turned up at County Hall and was escorted up the wide stone stairs from the lobby. Then up some more stairs. Corridors led off the landings towards open doors through which I saw computers, scruffy-looking desks, chairs with cardies slung over their backs. And another flight of stairs. By now there was lino underfoot.

Finally, we arrived at the fourth floor, where a large lobby was covered in wall to wall, sound-deadening Axminster. A marble bust on a plinth stood below a list, on brass, of officers who had died in World Wars I and II.

'The Committee rooms are up here,' explained the woman who was leading the way.

The Committee in this case was represented by three men, quite pleased with themselves. We sat in a boardroom at a long table and they suggested alternatives to driving that I might pay for myself. Like the train. I explained (again) that my daughter was mentally ill, volatile and impulsive. It would not be out of character for her to stroll across the track. Last year I'd sent them the crime reference number for the suicide threat in 2014 but they still hadn't understood.

After about an hour of to-and-fro over points that had already been made on both sides, the lead member was summing up against me. 'What we have to decide,' he intoned, 'is whether or not the circumstances of this child mean that she has no choice but to attend an out-of area school. As I understand it the original transfer was made at your request, Miss Mare, not that of Chloë's first school.

Therefore given that you chose this option, I'm afraid we—'

'No. Excuse me,' I said. This was my only chance to push back. 'You're implying that I had a choice between two equally attractive schools. I didn't. My choice was whether to make my thirteen-year-old daughter go back to a school where she'd been bullied so badly that she *threatened to commit suicide*. What would you have done if it'd been your suicidal child? Well?'

'I see your point,' murmured one of them. The others looked at their notebooks and muttered assent.

'Exactly. I chose *not* to make her go back there. My only option was an out of area school. She's been doing well there for nearly a year.'

In the New Year of 2017 she got her bus ticket. The driver understands how she is and she always rides in the single seat closest to him.

+++

2017

It's February now, and Chloë's school, the best one she's ever been at, has given up on her.

I knew she was unmanageable again. Just before she had to go back in January I drove her to the nearest Debenham's to get a school skirt. On the way, she told me she must have a pencil skirt.

I knew perfectly well that a pencil skirt would inspire a letter from her form teacher about the Rules, which were –Mid-Grey Knee-length A-line or Pleated Only. No circular, pelmet, midi, full, or straight skirts; no pinafore dresses. I wasn't going to waste my money on something that she'd wear once only to incite a stupid row.

'They won't let you wear it,' I said. 'It's got to be pleated or A-line.'

She started screaming. I had to stop the car. She jumped out and ran off across a field. Gemma, in the back in her baby seat, started to cry. Chloë disappeared through a spinney towards a housing estate and I rang the police. 'I can't run after her,' I said. 'I can't leave the baby.' A couple of young policemen turned up in a hatchback. 'She's gone into that estate,' I said, pointing. 'If you see her please don't run after her. Just bring her back. She's got psychiatric issues. If you run, she's impulsive and she might run into danger.' They set off in the hatchback and brought her back ten minutes later. It was a long ten minutes. Like most police teams, they thought she was just 'out of control'. She stood sullenly in front of them while they told her off.

From the start of the term she has been slamming out of classes. One Thursday she was seen leaving the premises and a teacher chased after her. I found out when I got a letter on Saturday morning. *Had it not been for Mr Taylor's swift pursuit of Chloë she would have been out of our control for longer. We really cannot ...*

'What's this about Mr Taylor running after you?'

'Oh, I lost him. I went back through the playing field.'

On the Monday morning I took her to school myself and insisted on seeing the Headmaster and Mrs Marshall together. I explained, carefully, the panic I felt when I read that Chloë had been chased.

'Do you know what can happen when you chase a girl with her condition?' They looked blank. 'I'll tell you, then. Anxiety is her main problem. She has to feel she's in total control. If you chase her, you threaten her. *She would jump off a high building rather than be caught.* Please understand this. She must not be chased.'

But there have been more incidents, more walkouts. They have imposed a 'fixed period exclusion.'

She's at home now. I have to find another school. We're already approaching GCSE exams.

Last Friday she met a friend after school and went to her house. I was going to pick her up at eight p.m. At seven, I got a call from the police. My daughter and her friend had been been found drunk in the town centre. There's a sort of pedestrian square there, with seats around trees. Apparently a security officer in Sainsbury's had seen two men talking to them and passing them bottles of Oasis, which is a fruit drink with enough sugar in it to disguise added vodka. Or, of course, rohypnol or even meths. This time it was probably vodka. The men melted away when the police car rolled in.

The police drove the girls to the police station and told them off. I arrived and brought Chloë home. She slept it off. She no longer goes out on her own.

Gemma, at two, understands that Chloë has to be approached warily. I've never told her to ask Chloë's permission before going into her room or touching anything of hers. She just does. The dogs have the same kind of sensitivity. They never go into a room when Chloë is there.

My whole life has shrunk, my options narrowed, since 2014. My daughter will be fifteen in May. Intellectually, she's bright in many ways. She could earn a living working with horses and maybe I will help her to start. But emotionally she's lost.

It would be easy to feel sorry for myself. Because of depression, my own eating has got out of control. I've got fat. It doesn't make me feel any better. I did have a consultation on the phone with a psychiatrist last year. I was told I had a kind of PTSD, grief and shock, rather like a bereavement. Only not. Because the little daughter I loved, who used to love me back, is still only just out of reach. I was prescribed anti-depressants but I won't take them. One medicated person in a household is enough. Anyway, there is no point in self-pity when I know that other people have coped for years with no advice, no prescriptions and no money, and their children are in a worse state than Chloë. You have to *push*.

I used to think that my children's health and education were my priorities; in other words, their future. Nowadays, my priority is stocking up with Concerta and Ritalin.

As to the future – I just don't know.